Korean Resources for Pastoral Theology

Korean Resources for Pastoral Theology

Dance of Han, Jeong, *and* Salim

JAMES NEWTON POLING

and HEESUN KIM

PICKWICK *Publications* · Eugene, Oregon

KOREAN RESOURCES FOR PASTORAL THEOLOGY AND CARE
Dance of *Han, Jeong,* and *Salim*

Pickwick Publications
An Imprint of Wipf and Stock Publishers
199 W. 8th Ave., Suite 3
Eugene, OR 97401

www.wipfandstock.com

ISBN 13: 978-1-60899-584-4

Cataloging-in-Publication data:

Poling, James N. (James Newton), 1942–

    Korean resources for pastoral theology / James Newton Poling and HeeSun Kim.

    vi + 128 p. 23 cm—Includes bibliographical references and index.

    ISBN 13: 978-1-60899-584-4

    1. Pastoral theology. 2. Theology, Practical—Korea (South). 2. Christianity—Korea (South). I. Kim, HeeSun. II. Title.

BR1328 P65 2012

Manufactured in the USA

Contents

Introduction

IN A TIME OF life-and-death challenges to the human spirit—global economics, nuclear dangers, environmental threats, and religious polarization and war—Christians must look for resources that provide new insights of God's power and care for all people. What are the forms of suffering and hope in the world today and how can Christians respond?

The Contributions of Korean Christian Churches

Korean Christians have unique contributions to make to our understanding of pastoral theology and counseling. Pastoral counselors and theologians from the United States should look to the South Korean Christian churches and other Asian churches for conversation partners about the nature of care and healing in today's world.

Our reflections in this book are based on our experiences in Korea and the United States. James Poling is a European American who has eighteen years of interaction with South Korean students, clergy, and church leaders, teaching and travel in Korea, and study of Korean religion and culture. HeeSun Kim is a Korean who has done academic work and ministry in Korea and the United States. From our experiences we believe there are life-giving perspectives in Korea that need to be shared with United States and Korean religious leaders who are searching for God's spirit at work for healing, liberation, and reconciliation.

What Is Pastoral Theology?

Christian pastoral theologians and counselors in the United States have produced some of the most creative ideas about the nature of human suffering and hope in the contemporary world. Experiments in new forms of Christian pastoral counseling started in the 1920s with Anton Boisen and Russell Dicks, who understood the promise of the new psychologies in dialogue with Christian theology and practices. In almost one hundred years these theologies and practices of care have spread over the world. Students from Asia, South America, Africa, Europe, and Australia have studied in the United States and transformed the vision of the healing processes in their local churches. Pastoral care specialists in many countries have likewise transformed the theories and practices of pastoral theology in the United States.

Pastoral theology, care, and counseling is a ministry practice and academic discipline arising from reflection on the church's ministries of care for persons, families and communities. Caring ministries are rooted in practices of the Christian church that emphasize healing, supportive community, and spiritual liberation in everyday life. Those of us who identify as pastoral theologians and caregivers seek resources that have practical value for sustaining people when their personal lives, their families and their culture face times of crisis. Pastoral Theology has a prophetic function as it gives public voice to the suffering needs of persons and families and develops a sustained critique of ideologies, institutions, and religious beliefs that oppress human persons and families.

Accountability of the Authors

For me (James Poling) as a European American Christian from the United States, Korea is not an easy culture to understand. I have many obvious limitations such as inadequate knowledge of Korean language, religion, history, and basic assumptions and worldview. The Korean language, for example, has few historical connections with English and other European languages, and loses much of its rich meaning when translated into English. In addition, the interreligious setting of Shamanist, Buddhist, Confucianist, and Taoist values and worldviews astounds my Western logic. Many of my previous assumptions about Korea have been shattered through my experiences in the last twenty years. Even after sustained and careful reflection I feel reluctant to write down my thoughts for fear of falling into conceptual traps that my mind has created to protect my fragile sense of competence. On the other hand, my faith and life have been profoundly changed by the South Korean people and culture, and thus I am compelled to write. I am motivated to write because of my fears and hopes for my children and grandchildren living in the midst of the United States society and religion that is dangerously adrift in the world. I am motivated by my desire to find truth, beauty, and justice to heal my own spiritual poverty. I have found something in Korean culture that is healing and salvific and it is time to share with others.

For me (HeeSun Kim) as a Korean woman, one of my burdens about writing this book was whether I might essentialize or overgeneralize the Korean culture. Since I am only one person, my perspective cannot represent Korea overall. At the same time, I live in a culture where I become essentialized and misrepresented because of my race, gender, and my "exotic" foreign accent. Before I came to the United States, I hardly regarded myself as Asian—I was just a Korean. My identity as Korean has developed many layers in the United States. I still cannot forget the moment when someone called me a "women of color" or "person of color." I was shocked and automatically looked at my skin to see "what color" I have. In the United States, I see myself situated in a complicated web. In many cases, Asian women in the United States become romanticized or misunderstood, and I have resisted those overgeneralized assumptions for many years. Yet, somehow in this book I am talking about Korea in general. Life is full of irony, I guess.

Talking about Korea, whether from a non-Korean's perspective or a Korean's perspective, means becoming bold and vulnerable at the same time. I can speak about my culture based on what I have experienced within limitations, and I also do not want to overgeneralize about Korea.

I wish I could wash my hands of these complications, claiming my innocence. But like Pilate, perhaps, I may be found guilty after all—as he is still being cited, "suffered under Pontius Pilate." I will take it as Karma. With all the risks, nevertheless, I still want to write about Korea if this book helps more people see some unique values of Korea and have *jeong* for the Korean people.

When we decided to work on this book together, it meant, for me, we were supposed to be open to being corrected, challenged, and encouraged by each other; and we did. And I expect the same thing from the conversation with the readers.

Why Korea?

Korea has a five-thousand-year history of religion and culture, and its identity and even existence was threatened in the twentieth century by encounters with Western modernity in the form of colonial military occupation, civil war and modernization. Beginning in the nineteenth century Japan was the first modern nation to pressure and then occupy Korea. At first Western nations encouraged Japanese expansion into eastern and southern Asia as a proxy for the empires of Europe and the United States. Later Japan was seen a threat to world peace. From 1895 to 1945, millions of Koreans were killed, starved, kidnapped, enslaved, and controlled for the sake of the Japanese Empire in Asia. After the Second World War millions of Koreans died in civil war and government oppression from 1945 to 1953. Though Korea was not an active collaborator in colonialism or World War II, the global powers divided the Korean people into north and south and have maintained that division until today. Families and communities were torn apart and many family members have not seen or heard from one another in over sixty years. Thousands of Koreans died fighting in North and South Korea, and thousands more have died from persecution and famine in North Korea. The Korean people have suffered enormously in the last 125 years, and every family bears the traumatic scars from this century of horror. The long-term effects of this history on North Koreans cannot be easily gauged because of the secrecy of its government.

South Korea has recently prospered on many levels—economics, politics, art, music, religion, education, research, technology, and global influence. South Koreans have been generous with the people of North Korea, sending supplies worth millions of dollars to alleviate the suffering of the people and offering an alternative future. This generosity has been criticized by some South Koreans and by politicians in the United States as appeasement and naïveté toward the communist north. Most important has been the sense of hope among the South Koreans.

We are interested in the actions of the spirit of the resilient God in the world. We see this resilient spirit in the South Korean people and culture. We want to know more about God's healing presence in the world. Can the world today be mended (*tikkun*, a Hebrew word for healing).[1] If so, the spirit of mending must be operative in the world. We believe God is calling South Korea (among other cultures and people) to express God's power for the mending of the world.

---

1. "The term *mipnei tikkun ha-olam* (perhaps best translated in this context as "in the interest of public policy") is used in the Mishnah (the body of classical rabbinic teachings codified circa 200 CE). There, it refers to social policy legislation providing extra protection to those potentially at a disadvantage—governing, for example, just conditions for the writing of divorce decrees and for the freeing of slaves" ("Tikkun Olam").

A Korean Vision

Our purpose in this book is to describe what we have seen and heard in Korea for the benefit of pastoral theology and care. What is the Korean vision and energy that can contribute to personal and global healing (*tikkun*)? If we can share what we have learned, perhaps our reflections will be a bridge for others who also seek healing for the world today.

To put our project in a more critical light, one could ask the following questions:

1. What are the important contributions that the South Korean people can make to pastoral theology and care in the United States?

2. Is South Korea just another modern state with all the contradictions of modernism that make the world dangerous for its peoples, cultures, and environment?

3. Does South Korea have a spirituality that transforms modernism into a kind of healing power that can be salvific for the world in the future?

There are no easy answers to these questions. However the question of healing for the world's cultures, peoples, and environment is so crucial that we have plunged ahead with our questions and search for answers. Many South Koreans have a spirituality that holds promise for the healing and salvation of the world. In our modest way we want to take this claim seriously and engage in searching for answers.

Outline of the Book

In order to explore the contributions of Korean spirituality, especially Korean Christian spirituality, to the United States and to international conversations, it is necessary to provide a historical, religious, and cultural introduction to Korea. While many congregations, religious leaders, and seminary communities in the United States have encountered the Christian passion and dedication of Korean individuals, the context of these encounters is distorted by several factors. First-generation Korean immigrants to the United States face many obstacles in communicating from their hearts: language, displacement from home, and economic challenges as well as the endemic white supremacy and ethnocentrism of most Christians in the United States. In spite of these obstacles, Korean Christians have made a significant impact on religious life in the United States. Whenever we join in any conversations about global Christianity, the witness of Korean Christians inevitably comes up. Christians in the United States are intrigued by their encounters with Koreans. Korean Christians have done a courageous job of interpreting themselves and their faith wherever they have gone.

A premise of this book is that United States Christians need to respond to the encounters with Korean Christians by meeting them halfway. This means the Christians in the United States need to study the history and culture of Korea and be prepared to support Korean Christians as they express their faith and develop their global mission.

Chapters 1 to 4 give summaries of the history and religious context of Korea for the benefit of United States Christians who want to respond respectfully and competently to their Korean colleagues. For those who have no background in ancient Asian history, the first chapter may be more difficult. We suggest that some might want to skip chapter one and proceed to the modern history in which there is more interaction between East and West. Those who want to study further can find other resources in the footnotes and bibliography throughout the book.

Chapter 5 provides a perspective on contemporary South Korea as it encounters modernism from the United States and Europe. Chapters 6 and 7 are constructive chapters that respond to the question: What is the Korean contribution to United States pastoral theology and pastoral care? We present several key ideas and discuss them in relation to the Christian theology. Several analogies give promise of mutual conversations between Korean and United States Christian pastoral theologians.

We invite you to join us on an intercultural and interreligious adventure that promises to have benefit for Christians in the United States and Korea and beyond to the glory of God and the salvation of the world.

1

Early History of Korea

IT IS DIFFICULT FOR many Westerners to understand Korean history and culture before the modern period. Part of the challenge of meeting Korean Christians halfway is encountering words and images that do not connect with a Western reader's experience. Because the shock of alterity or strange otherness can be disorienting, some readers may want to skim this chapter on the ancient history and skip to chapter two where the modern period is discussed.

Over many centuries, the people on the peninsula have engaged in interaction and conflicts with China, Russia, and Japan. Korea is a small nation surrounded by global superpowers that have buffeted its culture and everyday life. Its narrative has been distorted by its subordination to China in ancient times, and the false ideologies the Japanese used to justify their colonial oppression of Korea during the early twentieth century. United States culture has a long history of racial bias toward Asian immigrants that shapes the unconscious perceptions of many Western Christians. It is hard to overcome this history so that creative, mutually respectful conversation can occur.[1]

---

1. "Orientalism," a form of Western racial and cultural prejudice toward Asia takes two forms: devaluation of Asian cultures and peoples and romanticization of Asian cultures and people. Namsoon Kang states the romantic tendency clearly: "There are also Asia admirers—both specialist and amateur, both Asians and Westerners—who have the tendency to attribute to 'Asia' absolute differences from the West. They believe that 'Wisdom of the East' and its spirituality offer a deep, ancient, penetrating wisdom that will contribute to overcoming the 'destructive' materialism and individualism of the West. In such a form of anti-West-centrism, they merely change the evaluative connotation of this Oriental essence from negative to positive while keeping its cognitive content unchanged" (Kang "Confucian Familism," 170).

In the eighteenth and nineteenth centuries, many sensitive artists and intellectuals felt the profound crisis in Korea before it was fully apparent to everyone else. The crisis came because Korea's national autonomy was endangered by invasions from Japan, France, Britain, and the United States as they were expanding their trade and domination of weaker countries. In its starkest form, the question was this: If Korea lost control of its political, economic, intellectual, and religious institutions, what would happen to the people? Before this question even took public form, artists, religious leaders, and scholars began to search for the spiritual roots of Korean identity in the story of Dangun.

Chaeho Shin,[2] an early twentieth-century historian, helped lay the foundation for the recovery of Korea's ancient history by arguing that there was a spiritual Korean identity which he called *minjok* that would survive the colonial period.[3] He tried to lay out an ethnically (*minjok*) based linear national history of Korea that would not be distorted by the colonial perspective. Although Shin's ideas of a pure Korean ethnic identity were romantic, the search for the roots of a Korean culture that has survived modernism is important for Koreans. In this chapter, we review some of the earlier history of the country to provide a context for Western readers to enter the Korean narrative.

Ancient Korea: GoJoseon (2333—108 BCE)

Dangun (Tangun) was the legendary founder of the first Korean kingdom. The legend begins with his grandfather Hwan-in, the "Lord of Heaven" and Hwan-ung, his father.

> Hwan-ung descended to Mount T'aebaeksan on the border between Manchuria and what is now North Korea. He named the place Shinshi, City of God. Along with his ministers of clouds, rain, and wind, he instituted laws and moral codes and taught the humans various arts, medicine, and agriculture. A tiger and a bear . . . prayed to become human. Upon hearing their prayers, Hwan-ung called them to him and gave them 20 cloves of garlic

2. Shin and Robinson, *Colonial Modernity in Korea*, 356–61. Chaeho Shin (1880–1936) is also credited with inventing the term *minjung*, the oppressed majority. Chang, "Shin Chaeho's Nationalism."

3. In the 1940s, PomSuk Yi used the term *minjok* to refer to racialized purity that sounded uncomfortably close to Hitler's use of *volk* to mean Aryan racial purity. Cumings, *Korea's Place in the Sun*, 207.

and a bunch of mugwort. He then ordered them to only eat this sacred food and remain out of the sunlight for 100 days. The tiger shortly gave up and left the cave. However, the bear remained true and . . . was transformed into a woman. The bear-woman was very grateful and made offerings to Hwan-ung. However, lacking a companion she soon became sad and prayed beneath a sandalwood tree to be blessed with a child. Hwan-ung, moved by her prayers, took her for his wife and soon she gave birth to a handsome son. They named him Tan-gun, meaning "Altar Prince" or sandalwood. Tan-gun developed into a wise and powerful leader and in 2333 BC moved to P'yongyang and established the Go-Joseon ("Land of the Morning Calm") Kingdom. Finally, at the age of 1,908, he returned to T'aebaeksan where he became a mountain god.[4]

According to legend, since 2333 BCE, the Korean people have looked to the mountains for spiritual strength, lived in harmony with one another, and spread their culture far and wide. Eventually the Korean people filled the peninsula, spread into Manchuria, and immigrated to Japan and other areas. They were a religious people who respected the spirits that lived in the world alongside its people and engaged in rituals to the spirits that determined the destiny of families, kings, rain, agriculture, and periodic natural disasters such as floods, droughts, etc.

Korea is unusual in the world because beliefs and practices of the spirit religion (what some scholars call Shamanism) have survived through the centuries into the modern period. Half of Koreans do not confess any religion, and more than half are familiar with the services of *mudangs*, as female shamans are often called. Anthropologists have done many studies in Korea because there is a large active practice of shamans. One consequence of Korea's religious history is the vitality and intensity of its interreligious culture. "Many [Koreans] do not want to confine themselves to only one religious tradition. Instead they want to be free to visit shamans and Buddhist temples and participate in the activities of new religious organizations without being told that by doing so they [are] no longer permitted to participate in the rituals and worship activities of other religious communities."[5]

4. "The Legend of Tan-Gun" (http://www.lifeinkorea.com/information/tangun.cfm). Compare http://en.wikipedia.org/wiki/Dangun.

5. Baker, "Introduction," in Buswell, *Religions of Korea in Practice*, 3.

Three Kingdoms Period (57 BCE—668 CE): Goguryeo, Baekje, and Silla[6]

GoJoseon (2333–57 BCE)
Three Kingdoms Period (57 BCE—668 CE) [Goguryeo (37 BCE—668 CE), Baekje (18 BCE—660 CE) and Silla (57 BCE—935 CE)]
Unified Silla (668–935) and Balhae (698–926)
Goryeo (918–1392)
Joseon (1392–1910)
Japanese Colonial Period (1910–1945)
Republic of Korea, Democratic People's Republic of Korea (1948–present)

Goguryeo (37 BCE—668 CE) was located in Manchuria and the northern part of the peninsula: Baekje (18 BCE—660 CE) in southwestern Korea, and Silla (57 BCE—935 CE) in the southeast. Because these three nations coexisted, this is called the Three Kingdoms Period. Goguryeo established itself as a major power in the northern region, vying with China for control of Manchuria. With its expansion toward the north, Goguryeo emerged initially as the most powerful, largest and most advanced of the three kingdoms.[7] Baekje fostered high qualities of art, academic studies, science, and religion; and also played an important role in passing on its cultural heritage to Japan. Silla was a weaker nation than the other two nations but as its power grew strong, Silla made an alliance with China and finally succeeded in unifying all Three Kingdoms.[8]

Unified Silla (668–935 CE) and Balhae (698–926 CE)

The era of the Three Kingdoms came to an end when Baekje and Goguryeo were defeated by the combined forces of Silla and Tang from China. While Silla gained control of the southern part of the Three Kingdoms, it lost the northern part of Goguryeo. The descendants of Goguryeo established a new nation in the north section of the peninsula and Manchuria called Balhae (698–926). The Three Kingdoms era changed to the era of the Southern

6. Western readers will be helped in this section if they search maps of ancient Korea online. Type "ancient Korea" into a search engine.

7. Wright, *Korea: Its History and Culture*, 12.

8. Yoo, *The Discovery of Korea*, 28.

(Silla) and Northern (Balhae) States. The culture of Buddhism thrived during this period with the establishment of beautiful temples, pagodas and temple bells. The most representative shrines are the Bulguksa Temple and the Seokuram Grotto.

The cultural sites from Silla's old capital city of Gyeonju were created after the unification. The historic capital of Silla at Gyeongju is now a leading tourist attraction for Koreans and foreigners because the modern South Korean government has restored many of the temples, palaces, ancestral burial sights and other artifacts. The restoration features early scientific instruments in astronomy, world-class pottery, and magnificent traditional buildings. During the unified Korea under Silla, Shamanism, Buddhism, Confucianism, and Taoism lived in harmony and the country was at relative peace. Confucian classics, with their new ways of thinking, were introduced into schools. With advancements in technology, the lives of the people in Silla became more prosperous.

Balhae, in the north, recovered the former territories of Goguryeo, combining forces with the surrounding powers by the mid-eighth century. Balhae frequently traded with China and with Japan and opened transportation routes to Silla in the south, which referred to Balhae as the Northern State. The two nations exchanged diplomatic missions as well as trade activities. Two hundred twenty years after the Silla unification, the peninsula was once again divided: into the Later Three Kingdoms and the powers who proclaimed to be successors to Baekje and Goguryeo.[9]

Goryeo (918–1392 CE)

The earlier unification of the Three Kingdoms by Silla had been incomplete in that it did not include the ancient territories of Goguryeo, and it coexisted with Balhae in the north. The reunification of Korea by Goryeo, therefore, was more complete in that it encompassed the later Three Kingdoms and Balhae. Goryeo sought to reclaim all the territory once held in Manchuria by Goguryeo. A lively Korean community in Manchuria continues to this day. However, Goryeo suffered from invasions from China and thus many cultural properties were burned or destroyed during this time. The kings of Goryeo relied on Buddhism to consolidate its power, and many scholars

---

9. Cumings, *Korea's Place in the Sun*, 34–35.

believe that this patronage by the royal family contributed to the corruption of Buddhism.[10]

The capital of the northern kingdom of Goryeo capital was in Kaesong, in present-day North Korea near the thirty-eighth-parallel border. Struggles with the Mongols placed Goryeo in a crisis. With religious determination and faith in the Buddha, Goryeo undertook a woodblock carving of the Tripitaka Koreana, the sacred Buddhist scriptures, over a period of sixteen years, as a kind of supplication to prevent foreign invasion and defend the nation. "The first was completed in 1087 after a lifetime of work, but was lost; another, completed in 1251, can still be viewed today at the Haein-sa Temple . . . By 1234, if not earlier, Goryeo had also invented movable metal type, two centuries before its inception in Europe."[11]

Goryeo officially recognized Buddhism as the state religion, while using Confucianism as the principle of governmental practices. While Buddhism became the basis for cultivating one's mind, Confucianism became the principle of organizing and running the society. In this way Confucianism and Buddhism coexisted in Goryeo. By the end of the Goryeo period, Buddhism was losing its leading role in society and faced criticism.

At the end of the Goryeo period, a new bureaucratic class adopted Neo-Confucianism as the ideology and criticized Buddhism by calling for social reforms. The new literati dreamed of a new society, believing that the fate of Goryeo had come to an end. With SeongGye Yi came the establishment of a new dynasty of Joseon.

Goryeo allowed foreigners, including those from the Sung, the Khitan, the Jurchen, and Japan, to enter the state, and encouraged foreign trade. As a result, Goryeo became known as "Corea" to the Arabian merchants, who engaged in active trade activities around the world. Even though Goryeo perished, the name remained as *Korea*. North Korea identifies itself with Goryeo and has restored certain historical sites in Kaesong, which it shows off to pilgrims from South Korea.

Joseon (1392–1910 CE)

From 1392 to 1910, Korea was unified by the Joseon dynasty, which established the capital in Seoul in 1394. Joseon distanced itself from Buddhism and accepted Neo-Confucianism as the new moral system for its society. The

10. Lee, *Korean Language and Culture*, 61.

11. Cumings, *Korea's Place in the Sun*. 43–44.

reform toward Neo-Confucianism extended into metaphysics and cosmology (the view of ultimate reality and of the relationship of God to humans and the world), as well as into ethics, and into a commitment to extending its values into the everyday life of the common people. These changes promoted Confucianism as a world religion, not just a political philosophy. Emphasizing loyalty within families, village cooperation, and personal loyalty between subjects and kings, Joseon organized everyday Korean life much more thoroughly than it had been before. One of the problems of this total reorganization of society was the development of a more rigid gender hierarchy that restricted elite women to homes and oppressed women of the working classes. Modern feminists debate the origins of Korean gender inequality in today's South Korea and many blame Neo-Confucianism for the patriarchy that continues to exist in modern Korea. "In a Confucian society, women must subject their will to that of male members in a family. Throughout her life, a woman's duty is to follow the Tao of Three Obediences: before marriage, to obey her father, after marriage to obey her husband, and in the event of the husband's death, to obey her son. In the contemporary legal system, Koreans have inherited this Tao of Three Obediences in the form of restricting the headship of a family to male members, which prohibits women from assuming the legal headship."[12]

The penetration of Neo-Confucianism into daily life in some ways exceeded the influence of Neo-Confucianism in China. Korea has a history of incorporating and transforming outside influences, whether Buddhism, Confucianism, or Christianity, until its expression becomes authentically Korean. The Neo-Confucianism of Korea was articulated by Hwang Yi and Yi Yi, who formed competing factions. Their theories were disseminated to Japan, which greatly impacted the development of Neo-Confucianism in Japan. However, the metaphysics of Neo-Confucianism was difficult for the commoners to understand, and thus did not greatly affect their lives and was used mainly for political conflict among the ruling class.[13]

One aspect of the Neo-Confucian reform was the theoretical extension of citizenship to the common people, thus laying the basis for future debates about democratization. Every family was expected to practice filial piety within the family and to honor their ancestors through three generations (120 years). The contemporary Korean rituals that venerate ancestors and prescribe honorific language and behaviors such as bowing owe their

12. Kang, "Confucian Familism," 185.
13. Deuchler, *Confucian Transformation of Korea*, 231.

origin to this period. At the same time, some commoners who had never had a chance for literacy and education found new opportunities. A civil-service exam partially replaced family-of-origin criteria for government employment, thus potentially moving the nation toward a merit system of social opportunity rather than hereditary domination. Modern Korean commitment to education and rigorous testing practices may be rooted in this practice of the Joseon dynasty. Under Joseon, Neo-Confucianism was for everyone, and the government was bureaucratized so that nonelites had some chance of becoming *yangban*,[14] that is, part of the intellectual and political class.

The early years of Joseon involved exciting reforms and ushered in a time of expansion and optimism. However, late Joseon was characterized by regression on many of these reforms, a return to hereditary government and social status, and isolation from international influence. These internal problems meant that Korea was not prepared when confronted with pressure from modern empires that were looking for resources to exploit and ideologies to export.[15]

Encounter with Early Modernism[16]

Northern European empires forcefully entered Asia in the early sixteenth century. By 1619 Great Britain had colonies in India, Burma, Thailand, Australia, and Papua New Guinea. The Netherlands had colonial adventures in Indonesia, New Guinea and Japan, and Spain controlled the Philippines and other East Asian islands. None of these empires had a sustained presence inside Korea before the late nineteenth century but their presence in Asia had profound effects on Korean trade and intellectual exchanges.

14. The Joseon dynasty had four traditional social classes: *Yangban* (the elite, educated upper class), *Joong-in* (petit bourgeoisie), *Pyeongmin* (the commoners), and *Cheonmin* (those of low birth). See Wright, *Korea: Its History and Culture*. 51–52. See also Cumings, *Korea's Place in the Sun*, 52–53, for discussion of class in Korea.

15. Joe presents one of the strongest arguments for the corruption of the late Joseon dynasty (Joe, *Colonial History of Modern Korea*, 96–110).

16. Modernism is an intellectual, religious, political, and economic transformation arising out of eighteenth- and nineteenth-century Europe. Its definition is controversial and contested. For simplicity, we follow the lead of John B. Cobb Jr., who defines modernism as "economism," that is, the domination of global culture by market capitalism and a philosophy of individual freedom (Cobb, *The Earthist Challenge to Economism*). See further discussion in chapter 4.

The invasion of three hundred thousand Japanese troops into Korea in 1592 was a military threat for which Korea was not prepared. Japanese warlords had been fighting with one another for centuries and honing their skills in military technology and strategies. Korea had ignored its own military development in favor of administrative and intellectual development. After Japanese warlords were consolidated under the leadership of Toyotomi Hideyoshi, they turned their attention to international conquests, with Korea first on the list. Early in the conflict Pusan and Seoul fell and Koreans fled to the countryside where they organized local militia. Through extraordinary unity and courage, Korean ground forces led by Admiral Sun-Sin Yi with help from China (the Ming dynasty) repelled the Japanese. In a second Japanese attack in 1597 Korean and Chinese forces were again able to repel the Japanese after significant losses on both sides. China, controlled by the Manchus, invaded Korea in 1627 and 1636 and forced Korea to submit itself to the Chinese Manchu emperor of the Qing dynasty.

Almost fifty years of war left Korea in a vulnerable position because of losses of people and property. The government responded with a hermit attitude. Korea used its newly gained military skills to seal its borders to the outside world except for tributes to China and minimal trade with Japan. Unlike other East Asian nations, Koreans prevented most direct trade from European companies until the end of the nineteenth century. The contemporary isolation and independence of contemporary North Korea has strong historical precedence in these periods from the past.

Some scholars suggest that the Korean people are the most Confucianized in the world. If there is truth to this, it is because of the Joseon dynasty and Neo-Confucianism. All over the mountains of South Korea there are traditional Confucian ancestor graves where annual rituals of honor are performed during *Chusok* (a thanksgiving holiday in September). Other practices such as gift giving, lavish hospitality for guests, bowing, and honorific language probably come from the Joseon period; although these practices have a longer history among elites, with roots in feudal economies of reciprocity and tribute. In some ways, Joseon was a classic feudal system that survived until the nineteenth century. The Joseon kingdom presided for five centuries, but also made Korea vulnerable to the invasion of militaristic foreign nations. Due to the invasions, the politics and society underwent significant changes. Factional strife deepened and as one faction began to monopolize power, political abuses increased.

Catholicism, known in the eighteenth century as "Western Learning" (Silhak), introduced Korean scholars to Western intellectual culture. The Silhak thinkers liked the modern European emphasis on practical solutions to human problems for the common people and encouraged intellectual exchanges with Western thought and practices. Sustained contact with Western ideas began in 1784 with the conversion of SungHun Yi to Christianity in Beijing.[17]

In the aftermath of the significant changes that took place in Joseon society following the foreign invasions, Silhak scholars urged sweeping reforms to alleviate the hardships endured by commoners. The Silhaks were Confucian scholars who were influenced by modern thought in Roman Catholic literature that came to Korea from China, especially through Jesuit tracts and books. Some Silhaks were baptized and small Christian communities began to develop.

> Catholicism began to be disseminated in earnest in East Asia with the arrival of Francis Xavier in Japan in 1549 and especially with the arrival of Matteo Ricci in Beijing in 1601 . . . From [their] writings, many Koreans discovered a new worldview, one that posed an alternative to the Neo-Confucian orthodoxy of late Choson society. And, as is well known, it is through the study of these writings that a group of Koreans—first mostly from the elite yangban class but later also from the lower classes—took the initiative to form an indigenous Catholic community in Korea.[18]

However, regular persecution kept the numbers of Catholics small and forced the Christian movement underground. The Silhak scholars were especially concerned with the rigidity and isolation of Neo-Confucian thought during late Joseon.

---

17. "The history of Christianity in Korea is prefaced by a period of initial missionary endeavors, attempts made in the late sixteenth century and early seventeenth century by Catholics in Japan, China, and the Philippines to reach the population of the Hermit Kingdom . . . Although attempts to enter Korea to conduct missionary work were unsuccessful, many Korean scholars were aware of the teaching of the Catholic Church through pamphlets written by Jesuit missionaries . . . or by direct contact with missionaries in China . . . It was . . . 1784 when . . . Yi Sunghun accompanied his father to Beijing, made contact with the priests there, was baptized, and upon his return to Korea evangelized his friends" (Grayson, "Quarter-Millennium," in Buswell and Lee, *Christianity in Korea*, 8–9).

18. Kwang, "Human Relations," in Buswell and Lee, *Christianity in Korea*, 29.

The major concern of the *Sirhak* scholars was to illuminate the history and contemporary workings of political, economic, and social institutions. First preparing the ground by painstaking scholarly inquiries, they proceeded to elaborate their visions of how an ideal society might be achieved. By no means limiting their scholarship to fields of social science, such as politics and economics, they extended their inquiries to embrace many other areas—Chinese classical studies, historiography, geography, natural science, agriculture, and many more. Although the objects of their study were many and diverse, there was a common ground on which all Silhak scholars stood. Namely, the point of departure for their studies was the actual manifestation of things, their reality . . . Since the realities with which they were concerned were precisely those confronting their society in their time, their thought inevitably had a Korea-centric thrust to it.[19]

Scholars became engaged in studies to resolve issues of the everyday realities of the Korean people. However, Silhak scholars had various views for resolving the problems. Some advocated the importance of agriculture and urged reforms in the land system so that the farming land could be reasonably shared among farmers. Others called for mass production by developing the commercial and industrial sectors. Some called for the acceptance of the civilization of the Ching dynasty in China.

Had the Silhak intellectual and religious movement been received with more interest among other scholars and political leaders, perhaps Korea would have been better prepared for the explosion of new ideas a hundred years later. As it was, some scholars of the late nineteenth century recognized their debt to these courageous reformers who suffered for their ideas and faith.

In this chapter we have reviewed some of the earlier history of Korea. In the following chapter we look at Korea's encounter with modern Western ideas and nations to understand the contemporary situation.

19. Eckert et al., *Korea, Old and New,* 165.

2

Modern History of Korea

The Nineteenth Century

DURING THE LATE NINETEENTH century, Western nations forced the Joseon leaders to begin opening their borders for trade and influence. In reaction to the aggressive designs of the Westerners, as well as their different customs and cultures, the Joseon government tried to close its doors more tightly. In the nineteenth century, Korea was often called the Forbidden Land and the Hermit Kingdom[1] because it resisted the modern military, economic, and intellectual invasions of Western empires. It is not an accident that Japan was the brutal invader of Korea since the Japanese had interaction with Western empires for several centuries before Korea. When Europe, the United States, Russia, and Japan decided that Korea would be opened up to modernism by force, Korea was unable to defend itself and unprepared for the intellectual revolution that would be required. Daewongun, the regent, and the Kim family clan from Andong, who together dominated middle and late nineteenth-century Joseon, preferred isolation from Western influence, even as European and United States warships were prowling the coast of Korea. The drastic changes that reshaped Korea into modern states can be traced to the traders and naval forces of the United States (1853, 1871), France (1866), and Japan (1876), who persistently pressured Korea to join the international trading community.

1. Joe, *Cultural History of Modern Korea*, 145. "Korea was known long before the nineteenth century as a country where foreigners were met with mistrust and dispatched as quickly as possible back to their homes" (Cumings, *Korea's Place in the Sun*, 87).

How did the Korean intellectual and religious leaders respond to the pressures from modern empires? During the last years of the nineteenth century, indigenous religious and political movements emerged and called for social reforms. Many of these movements were short lived but a few had a significant historic impact on Korea. The most important of these new indigenous religions was *Donghak* (Eastern Learning), which distinguished itself from *Silhak*, or Western Learning of the nineteenth century.

Donghak Nationalism

The Donghak reform movement was initiated by Je-u Choe (1824–1864). In a personal experience of ecstasy and revelation, Choe was convinced that he had new insight into the nature of reality. He started writing and teaching a new religion. Choe's basic writings drew on insights of the traditional Korean religions as interpreted by the Silhak scholars. Donghak was based on the doctrine of the equality of all people and the unity of God with human beings. In addition to the religious aspect, the Donghak movement called for national stability and security. Choe's legacy survived persecution and his beheading by the government in 1864. His writings became scriptures for new Korean religions that have survived into the contemporary period and have many offshoots, one of which renamed itself Chondogyo.[2]

One result of the Donghak movement was the Peasant Revolution of 1894, led by BongJun Jeon, in which an indigenous army from southwestern Korea threatened the Joseon government in Seoul. Chinese and Japanese military forces joined with the Korean government and destroyed the rebellion. In the aftermath of this violence, Japan was able to increase its domination of the Korean government, leading eventually to full occupation and colonization by 1910.

The Donghak movement is seen by some scholars as a creative response that helped preserve Korean spirituality in the crisis of modernity facing Korea. Even though the Donghak peasant army was defeated, the resistance of the peasant movement had great significance as an event that demonstrated knowledge of modern concepts, called for reforms in the government and society, and opposed foreign domination. It can be seen as a precursor to the democratization movements of the nineteenth century.[3] Some historians blame the Donghak movement for internal strife that

2. New religious movements such as Chondogyo will be discussed in chapter 4.

3. "Tonghak . . . was by far the most important event in modern Korean history. It

made Korea vulnerable to Japanese domination and resulted in the end of Korean autonomy until 1945.[4] The Donghak influence will show up again in chapter four on Korean spirituality.

The Western Protestant Missionary Movement

When Gojong became Joseon King in 1863 and Daewongun, his father, was the regent, the government became more open to Christianity. At the same time a treaty forced on Korea by the United States established trading and opened the door to the missionaries and merchants.

When the first Protestant Christian missionaries (Horace Grant Underwood, Horace Allen, Henry Appenzeller, and others[5]) arrived in Korea in 1884 they were concerned with what they saw, especially the conditions of poor people, the oppression of women, and the lack of Western education and health care. To the eyes of many missionaries, the Korean people needed the Western enlightenment of the gospel, science, and capitalism. They set about converting persons and organizing institutions to transform the country. They immediately started schools, hospitals, and churches among men and women of all social classes. Some of these schools and hospitals later became elite institutions in modern Korea: Severance Hospital (now part of Yonsei University) in 1885, and Ewha Woman's University in 1886. Yonsei University's current motto is, "the first and the best." Of course this statement neglects the long history of Confucian schools (*suwon*) that have been central to Korean life for centuries.[6] Sungkyunkwan University, for example, traces its founding to the Goryeo dynasty in 1398. In addition,

---

signified the beginning of the modern era for Korea in that in Tonghak the equality of all people, the ideological underpinnings of modern democracy, was specifically declared as its basic creed. This was a climax of the prolonged democratic ferment, through political and social change, that spurred the rise of the common people and the Sirhak and Christian movements . . . In the end the force that Tonghak represented in its defiance of the ruling group and foreign powers prevailed, though at almost an intolerable cost" (Joe, *Cultural History of Modern Korea*, 96). See also *Focus on Korea*, 82.

4. Cumings, *Korea's Place in the Sun*, i, 115–20.

5. "Lilas Horton, M.D., later to become Mrs. Horace Grant Underwood, arrived in 1888 to act as physician to the queen of Korea" (Lafayette Avenue Presbyterian Church, "LAPC Story").

6. Sungkyunkwan University in Seoul is the leading Confucian school in modern Korea. "Old Sungkyunkwan was founded over 600 years ago by royal decree to promote the scholarship in Confucianism" (Sungkyunkwan University webpage http://www.skku.edu/eng/).

Buddhism has been training monks in Korea since the fifth century BCE. Christianity became one of the promoters of the philosophy of modernism in Korea, and with some notable exceptions, was founded with the prejudice that Korean religions and beliefs had little to contribute to the Korean people or to Christianity.[7]

The ideas of modernism had already been debated for two hundred years through the Silhak and the Donghak movements, and the persecution of Christians had pretty much run its course. In contrast to the Catholics of a hundred years earlier, Protestant missionaries were hospitably received. A member of the royal family and nephew of Queen Min, YoungIk Min, was severely injured in an attack on the palace, and Dr. Horace Allen provided medical treatment that saved his life.[8] As a result the royal family permitted Christian missionaries to work in Korea and gave them land and financial support to promote their institutions. Protestant Christians worked especially with the poor and with women who were ready for new opportunities for their families, and some of the people responded to the chance for education and healthier and more prosperous daily lives.

From its beginning in 1884 till 1910, the Protestant church grew to about two hundred thousand members. By 1960 there were one million Korean Christians in spite of the oppression of the Japanese occupation from 1910 to 1945, the division of Korea, and the Korean War, which made evangelistic work very difficult. Eighty percent of Korean Christians lived in North Korea before 1950, and many fled to the south during the war,

---

7. "This chapter also argues that the contents of these [Protestant] texts do not support the stereotypical view that early Protestant missionaries' attitude toward East Asian religious cultures was unfailingly and unremittingly imperialistic, bent on a total supplantation of traditional religions. Granted, the texts reveal that almost all of the missionaries held paternalistic attitudes toward East Asian religions—and some of them were unremittingly imperialistic; yet they also reveal that many missionaries made bona fide efforts—within the scope of their ultimate commitment, to be sure—to look favorably on local religions" (in Sung-Deuk Oak, "Early Protestant Literature and Early Korean Protestantism," in Buswell and Lee, eds., *Christianity in Korea*, 72).

8. "Horace Newton Allen (1858–1932), a Protestant, medical missionary from the United States, who later also served as a diplomat, made a remarkable impact on his mission country, Korea, where he arrived in 1884. He was the first Protestant missionary to work in the country. In 1885, he established Korea's first modern medical facility, Gwanghyewon, which has grown into the Yonsei University Severance Hospital and School of Medicine. In 1887, he accompanied Korea's first diplomatic delegation to Washington. He also wrote some of the first books introducing Korean culture to the western world." ("Horace Newton Allen").

leaving behind family members, churches, and ancestral lands.[9] Even more phenomenal growth of Christianity in Korea occurred from 1960 to 1995, when the Christian church grew to 13 million[10] or 26.3 percent of the South Korean population.[11]

South Korea: Religious Makeup			
Religion	1985	1995	2005
Christian	20.7%	26.3%	29.2%
Roman Catholic	4.6%	6.6%	10.9%
Protestant	16.1%	19.7%	18.3%
Buddhist	19.9%	23.2%	22.8%
Confucian	1.2%	0.5%	0.2%
Other	0.8%	0.8%	0.8%
No Religion	57.4%	49.3%	46.9%
Source: National Census Bureau			
Note: Columns may not equal 100% because of rounding.			

Scholars debate the reasons for Christianity's rapid growth. They suggest that the Christian movement has been indigenous since the first Korean converts to Catholicism founded a Roman Catholic church on the peninsula in the eighteenth century. Protestant missionaries encouraged indigenization (the Nevius method) from the early days of mission work in the nineteenth century. The Christian emphasis on education and healing through schools and hospitals appealed to the Confucian tradition of solving practical problems and emphasizing education. Indigenous Christian leaders engaged in resistance to Japanese colonialism. While the influence of Christianity is morally ambiguous, important prophets of the Christian churches are honored today because they aligned with the common people in their struggles for justice during Japanese occupation. The United States military helped South Korea during the civil war with North Korea, and

9. Rhodes, *History of Korea Mission* 2:209–10.

10. *CIA World Factbook*; online: https://www.cia.gov/library/-publications/the-world-factbook/print/ks.html, 2008.

11. Lugo and Grim, "South Korea's Coming Election Highlights Christian Community"; online: http://pewresearch.org/pubs/657/south-koreas-coming-election-highlights-christian-community/. The chart on the religious makeup of South Korea is on this webpage.

subsequently the United States provided significant financial support of the developing Korean economy and government. All these factors have created a positive alliance between the Korean and United States governments in a way that strengthened the Christian churches in Korea.

A common saying in Korea is this: "There are three kinds of Korean Christians: conservative, very conservative, and extremely conservative." Most Korean Protestant Christians believe in Reformed doctrines about individual sin, personal salvation, heaven and hell, and the exclusive role of Jesus Christ as savior of the world. Most Korean Christians are pro-Western (especially pro-United States) in their politics; for example, many endorse free-market capitalism. Most Korean Christians are opposed to interreligious cooperation or openness with other religions. While one can detect Confucian influences such as filial piety and gender hierarchy among Christians, these same values have strong support among conservative Christians around the world. Christian scholars who advocate inter-religious understanding, cooperation, and appropriation of indigenous religious practices have to be careful what they say in local churches about traditional Korean religions, or they might alienate their audience and cause their ideas to be rejected. A friend told me (James Poling) a story about how he showed in a local Sunday school class a video that included an interview with a Christian who worked at a Buddhist university. While the subject of the video was not religious, someone in the class objected to use of the video because it promoted the validity of Buddhism.

It is not hard to find Christian leaders who believe that Christianity is the key to the future of county. Some leaders have said to me (James Poling) that Christianity is necessary because of the failure of Buddhism and Confucianism to offer the people any future. Even as the growth of Protestant churches has stalled in the last ten years, most Korean Christians believe that Christianity is the only possible future for Koreans. Ironically, the last twenty-five years have seen a resurgence of intellectual and popular interest in Buddhism, Confucianism, and Shamanism. On Buddha's birthday in 2008, I (James Poling) watched a Buddhist parade down one of the main streets of Seoul. Newspapers estimated that thirty thousand people representing various temples, universities, and other Buddhist programs participated in this annual celebration, giving the impression that Buddhism is anything but fading. Many of the most beautiful and sacred sites in Korea are Buddhist temples that thousands, whether they are Buddhist or not, visit on a regular basis. Buddhism has positioned itself as a conserver of the ancient history. Christianity has certainly transformed Korea through the growth of its churches, hospitals, universities, global missionary movement, and many other programs, but it may not have adapted fully to its role in a religiously pluralistic society.

Nineteenth-Century Trauma and Transformation

Most scholars agree that Korean society was not prepared for the invasion of European and Japanese military forces, the power of modern ideas, and Western plans for domination of the peninsula. Some scholars understand Korea's vulnerability purely as a matter of military strength. A small country on the international stage, Korea could not likely have withstood the military invasion of the global empires at the end of the nineteenth century. In fact it is remarkable that it remained a hermit kingdom as long as it did. "Imperialism, Japanese style, with its falsehood, robber baronial greed, and murderous instinct finally caught up with Korea, which, having been engrossed in the practice of peaceful coexistence for so long, would be hard put to handle a military nation whose time had come."[12]

The Japanese dominated for decades not only Korea but also much of China, Taiwan, Indonesia, and other countries of Asia. Had they not overreached their power when they attacked the United States at Pearl Harbor, the Japanese might still be the dominant military force of East Asia.

But was it a purely military imperialism that endangered Korean national autonomy?

Much of the nineteenth century was a time of oppression and trauma for the Korean people. As Western empires sent military forces, traders, and missionaries to "open up Korea," the ideas of modernity began to flow in. We have described the intense debate between more conservative scholars of Neo-Confucianism and Donghak scholars. This debate may have prepared the way for Japan to increase its influence in Korea not just as an imperial power, but also as a force for modern ideas and politics.[13] The United States and Japan were allies through much of the nineteenth

---

12. Joe, *Cultural History of Modern Korea*, 170–71.

13. "Upon the opening of Korea to the outside world, the forces which had been unleashed in the Confucian northwestern Asia through the destruction of the traditional order of things by the self-righteousness West, plunged the countries in the region into a veritable 'vortex' of the ugliest international power play" (Joe, *Cultural History of Modern Korea*, 173).

century, and the Treaty of Portsmouth in 1895 defined the boundaries between their growing empires. The United States could colonize the Philippines without interference from Japan, and Japan could control Korea without interference from the United States. As Japan increased its control of Korean politics and economics, the United States honored its treaty with Japan and refused to support the exiles who brought many complaints to world bodies about the loss of Korean autonomy.[14]

Japanese colonization was a personal, political, and economic disaster for most families, in spite of the construction of an infrastructure of roads, railroads, and factories that helped fuel the later economic expansion. In addition to appropriating the agricultural products and laborers for its expanding war effort, the Japanese empire systematically attacked the symbols of Korean cultural and religious identity. It forced Japanese-language textbooks in the schools, required Koreans to change their names to Japanese ones, and appropriated or destroyed many historical records and artifacts so that Korea would become part of Japan. The apparent intent was to destroy any cultural and historical memory that Koreans had of themselves as a separate and independent people.

The most egregious violation of human rights was certainly the "Comfort Women," who were kidnapped and forced into brothels to service Japanese soldiers. One hundred thousand to two hundred thousand young girls and women were kidnapped and forced into this "service to the Empire." A majority of these women died before returning home to Korea. A small number of survivors and their supporters continue to demonstrate weekly at the Japanese embassy in Seoul.[15] They demand that the Japanese government tell the truth about what happened and pay restitution to the families of the women whose lives were destroyed through this sex trafficking.[16] The Japanese government has refused to formally apologize or pay restitution for this violation of human rights.

14. The Treaty of Portsmouth, New Hampshire, between Japan and the United States in 1895 granted the US control of the Philippines after the Spanish-American War. In exchange, the US agreed to the Japanese colonization of Korea. For most of the early twentieth century, Japan and the US were allies in dividing up economic access to east Asia until Japan overextended its reach and underestimated the US response that led to the Pacific campaigns of World War II (see Cumings, *Korea's Place in the Sun*, 141–42).

15. I (James Poling) joined the "Comfort Women" in their demonstrations at the Japanese embassy in Seoul on one occasion.

16. Kim, *enno no guntai to Chosenjin ianfu* [The emperor's army and the Korean comfort women. Soh, *Comfort Women*; Cumings, *Korea's Place in the Sun*, 179–80. See also Keller, *Comfort Woman: A Novel*.

The Protestant churches have engaged in a spirited debate over their role during the Japanese colonization of Korea from 1910 to 1945. Some important Korean Christians and missionaries from the United States supported resistance to Japan and provided sanctuary for the resistance movements. Some Christian schools were closed because they refused to adopt the Japanese language and curriculum and to incorporate Shinto worship into their programs. "Christian opposition to the Japanese is both a fact and a legend. The churches were sanctuaries in times of violence, like that of the 1919 independence movement, and many Western missionaries encouraged underdog and egalitarian impulses."[17] Some Korean Christians were martyred because they refused to offer homage at the Shinto shrines set up by the Japanese authorities.[18] One dramatic story is told about how the Japanese police took control of the Presbyterian General Assembly meeting in Pyongyang in 1938 and forced the delegates to approve of Shinto shrine worship as a patriotic act that they claimed was not religious.[19]

The Japanese government put pressure on churches, threatening to close the mission schools. Since many of the missionaries were the leaders of schools, they struggled over what to do. In 1938 two missionaries debated the issue. G. S. McCune, the principal of Soongsil School in Pyongyang, opposed the shrine worship, citing, "Thou shall not worship any other gods before me," while H. H. Underwood, the principal of Yonhee School in Seoul, said, "Give to Caesar what is Caesar's." As a result, Soongsil School had to close and its president, McCune, had to resign, while Yonhee school (now called Yonsei University) remained open.[20]

By 1938, due to the persecution and ambivalence, the majority of Korean churches had been forced to participate in Shinto shrine worship. Only a small number of Christian churches, along with a few foreign missionaries, kept resisting. The resisters were severely persecuted by the Japanese government.

Other missionaries were pro-Japanese and supported the domination of the Korean peninsula by the Japanese government. One reason may be because the United States was pro-Japanese during most of the Japanese imperial expansion before World War II. "The American missionaries,

17. Cumings, *Korea's Place in the Sun*, 157.

18. Kim, *Ju Gi-Cheul: The Life of the Reverend Soyang Ju Gi-Cheul, Lamb of Jesus*.

19. Chung, *Church Growth and Preaching*, 67–91.

20. See ch. 9, section 2, "The Shinto Shrine Worship," in *Han-guk Gidokgyo e Yeoksa* 2:285–331.

sharp and interested observers of the political development and generally of the pro-Japanese sentiment, foresaw, probably after the Russo-Japanese War, the fall of the Korean kingdom vis-a-vis the imperial aspirations of Japan. After a period of vacillation and rationalization, they cautiously began to welcome the Japanese 'advancing' to Korea and carefully and then openly cooperated with them. Surprising though it may seem, there were few missionaries who could be excepted from this delineation of the missionary profile in this period."[21]

Many of the historical and cultural records and artifacts have never returned from Japan to Korea and continue to be housed in Japanese museums and libraries. Japanese history textbooks insist, even today, that Korea was originally a vassal of Japan during the Silla dynasty and that colonization was justified as a means of returning Korea to its original and correct identity as part of Japan. In 1945 Korea was liberated from Japanese colonial occupation.

At the end of World War II, to which Korea was not a party, Russia and the United States divided the peninsula at the thirty-eighth parallel as the cold war began. Russia turned over control of North Korea to the military resisters who had fought Japan in Manchuria before the war. Kim Il-Sung emerged as the leader and installed the Marxist-Leninist government that remains in power today. Sadly, the Korean people were not allowed to establish a unified Korean government, and with the inauguration of two separate governments with different political ideologies, confrontation and conflicts between the two Koreas became a political reality.

The United States military controlled South Korea after 1945, during which time many South Koreans protested against United States control and were brutally put down by United States military troops.[22] Thousands died and suffered during this period. In 1948, the Republic of Korea (ROK) was formed under the leadership of Syngman Rhee. When he assumed power, President Rhee used his military to control the rebellious population under the guise of anti-Communism. The either/or logic of the cold war prevented a sophisticated analysis that could have fostered the genuine democratic demands of the people rather than the ideologies of infiltration and terrorism of Russian-inspired communists.

21. Joe, *Cultural History of Modern Korea*, 555: "Missionaries as Accomplices in the Japanese Enslavement of the Korean People."

22. Cumings says that the story of Korean local rebellion against United States military control has never been fully told (*Korea's Place in the Sun*, 139–41).

On June 29, 1949, the United States army withdrew its active troops, assuming that the South Korean army could defend its territory. On June 25, 1950, the North Koreans sent a massive army across the thirty-eighth parallel and within weeks had advanced to the outskirts of the city of Pusan on the southern tip of the peninsula. A surprise invasion by United States troops into the port of Incheon stopped the North Koreans from quick victory. United States and South Korean troops cut off the supply lines from North Korea and by early October 1950, South Korean and United States troops had pushed the North Korean army back to the thirty-eighth parallel. The war could have ended at this point because the thirty-eighth parallel actually became the armistice line, three years later, which endures until today. In October 1950, there were approximately five thousand United States deaths, and tens of thousands of North and South Korean deaths of soldiers and civilians.[23]

The decision of the United States to advance into northern Korea led to a massive destruction of people, buildings, and resources over the next three years. When the United States and allied forces reached the border of Korea with China at the Yalu River, the Chinese government entered the war with thousands of troops, surprising the South Korean and United States troops and resulting in massive casualties on both sides. By the end of the war, fifty-five thousand United States soldiers and several million Korean and Chinese soldiers and civilians had died. Massive bombing of North Korea by the United States leveled practically every building north of the thirty-eighth parallel. The fifty-eight-year history of isolation and paranoia in North Korea must be understood against this background of destruction. What now seems like paranoia by the North Korean political leaders is based on the memory of United States destructive actions in the early 1950s.

In 1960, the per capita income of South Korea was $1 per day. Adults who remember that period report hunger, illness, deaths, and many hardships. After the Armistice, the United States poured massive recovery aid into South Korea to help it in exchange for a promise that Korea would become a reliable ally in the cold war.

During the early years of the Republic of Korea, the United States supported dictatorial governments. The Rhee administration focused on reconstructing war-devastated South Korea and emphasized an anticommunist

---

23. For various views on twentieth-century Korean political and social history, see Cumings, *Korea's Place in the Sun*. Oberdorfer, *Two Koreas*. Lee, *New History of Korea*.

policy, while secretly pursuing plans for long-term rule. Many students and other citizens rose up in protest, but the police attempted to crush the protests by force. Amid a chaotic political situation upon Rhee's death, General ChungHee Park established a military government in 1961.

The Park government promoted policies of modernization and anti-Communism, and actively implemented growth-oriented economic plans. To achieve its goal, the government implemented a series of five-year economic development initiatives. As a result, Korea's economy grew tremendously. Its economic achievement was called the "Miracle on the Han River," named after the river that flows through the capital, Seoul. Park's government hoped that this occasion would help it prepare for long-term political control. Park transformed the presidency into a legal dictatorship, which prevented democracy from developing.

As a result of these actions, students, political activists, and the press started resistance movements against Park's government. The democratic movement was strongly oppressed by the government, which mobilized police forces to break down the protests. When ChungHee Park was assassinated in 1979, sadly, a new military power group by DooHwan Jeon seized the government. On May 18, 1980, in Gwangju, a massive demonstration against the military dictatorship was brutally oppressed by the police force. The government estimated that 144 civilians and forty-six military persons were killed in the incident. Other estimates range from 250 civilian deaths to over two thousand. The Gwangju Democratization Movement (also called the Gwangju uprising or massacre) is memorialized in a solemn park and public cemetery.[24] During this time military forces killed many people who were demonstrating against the government in other cities. Koreans who remember those times know the saying, "The democracy of Korea grew out of people's blood." The democracy of Korea is indebted to many innocents who died. Indeed, the Korean people were engaged in a great political struggle against tyranny and dictatorship.

Minjung theology emerged out of the encounter with sociopolitical injustices of the 1970s. *Minjung*, which means "people" or "commoners," refers to the social, political, and economic suffering of people throughout Korea's history. KwangSun Suh defines *Minjung* Theology as "a Korean theology. *Minjung* is a term which grew out of the Christian experiences in the political struggle for justice over the last thirty years. It is a theology of the oppressed in the Korean political situation, a theological response

---

24. Cumings, *Korea's Place in the Sun*, 382–86. Orberdorfer, *Two Koreas*, 124–32.

to the oppressors, and a response to the Korean church and its mission."[25] ByungMu Ahn identifies *minjung* with the Greek word *ochlos* in the Gospel of Mark, "a class of society which has been marginalized and abandoned."[26]

Han, a significant concept in *Minjung* theology, is an accumulation of suppressed and condensed experiences of oppression. Thus, according to Jiha Kim, "accumulated *han* is inherited and transmitted, boiling in the blood of people."[27] Despite the suppression of the human rights movement by Christian leaders, many Christians decided to remain in the church and hoped that the church would be for/with the *minjung*. They believed that the church should try to resolve the *han* of the *minjung* because that would be what Jesus would do in those times. *Minjung* theology greatly affected the social movements in those struggling times, consoling and inspiring many suffering people.

Successive political dictatorships undermined the development of democracy in Korea. However, the democratization movements organized by students and citizens in the last decades of the twentieth century contributed greatly to the democratic development. Because of increased demonstrations and pressures on the government, democracy finally came to South Korea in 1987. The economy of Korea continued to grow with the ups and downs of global capitalism. By 2008, the per-capita annual income was nearly $25,000 and $30,000 in 2010. The dramatic change in fortunes from 1910 to 2010 is one of the most remarkable economic stories of the last century.

The multiple crises of colonization, military dictators, civil war, and transformation from a rural, agricultural economy to an urban, industrialized, technological society dedicated to market capitalism has been traumatic for the South Korean people. This is the context in which the many forms of Korean religion must be understood.

South Korean Christians disagree in their evaluations of the history of twentieth-century Korea. The church is divided between those who promote social justice for all social classes, and those who promote a prosperity gospel; between those who want to encourage interreligious cooperation and transformation, and those who see non-Christian religions as superstitious and empty rituals; between those who encourage self-criticism of the church's role in promoting gender, race, and class oppression, and those

25. Suh, "Biographical Sketch of an Asian Theological Consultation," 16.

26. Ahn, *Jesus of Galilee*, 121–23.

27. Suh, "Towards a Theology of Han," 64.

who defend the church against such secular humanistic arguments. Many ideas and practices are contested within Korean Christianity today as they have been throughout Korean history. As we shall see later, contesting ideas may be a sign of a postmodern vision that is coming into being in Korea for the benefit of all humanity.

In the next chapter, we look at the larger interreligious context of Korea as a background for understanding Korea today.

3

Ancient Korean Religions

IN THE LAST CENTURY and a half, Korean society has experienced traumatic violence and destruction. Japanese and Western empires destabilized the national and local governments. Japanese colonization, world war, and civil war caused massive migration and forced workers to distant places. Since the end of the Korean War in 1953, cold war, capitalism, and urbanization have dramatically impacted every person. Extended South Korean families who, for centuries, lived together in villages and small cities have moved to high-rise apartment buildings in megacities and most people work in wage-oriented jobs. In 2010, Seoul at 20,550,000 was the second-largest city in the world.[1] Nearly everything that was familiar about Korea in 1900 has been destroyed and transformed. The few traditional houses and villages left are now sites of curiosity rather than the economic backbone of the nation.

In the midst of this violent and disorienting change, South Korean society has one of the most vibrant interreligious cultures in the world. Multiple world religions exist side by side with cults and new religious movements in an unusual mixture of conflict and tolerance. Within many extended families, one can discover beliefs and practices from Shamanism, Buddhism, Confucianism, Taoism, and Christianity. To understand the Korean people, one must know something about their religious history and current configuration. If we can understand the country's interreligious reality, perhaps we will discern the deeper pluralism that is becoming characteristic of the postmodern global reality for all human beings.

1. Tokyo, Japan (32,450,000); Seóul, South Korea (20,550,000); Mexico City, Mexico (20,450,000); New York City, USA (19,750,000); Mumbai, India (19,200,000); "Largest Cities of the World."

Many religions coexist in South Korea. For example, a casual walk through the busy streets of Seoul can prove to be a religious studies lesson of itself. Passing by many local shops of fortune-telling shamans, you take the stairs down to the subway station. At the ticket booth, you might come across a Buddhist monk, asking for alms for the local temple. Your train comes and you are fortunate enough to find a seat. Once you've settled in, you notice a group of conservative Christians passing out pamphlets and church bulletins. Some might have brought with them a big sign that says, "Jesus = Heaven, All Else = Hell." If you stay for a long enough ride, you may realize that the person sitting next to you wants to share the gospel in a more relational manner, asking you whether you are interested in becoming a new person in Christ. You often notice that young people yield their seats when elderly persons come near their seats, which is a Confucian virtue. On your way out of the subway and as you take the escalators up to the ground level, another individual may tap you on your shoulder, asking "Do you want to know about the Way/Truth?" This person may be a member of Daesunjinrihoe, one of Korea's new religions. If you show interest, you may be invited to a home where you'll partake in rites to resolve your ancestor's *han*. It is not over yet. Still, you can be accompanied by myriad followers and leaders of various religions on the streets. Look: there's a Catholic priest walking over there, and a group of nuns waiting in line for the bus . . . Truth. The Way. Salvation. You may reach the answer faster when you come to Korea. Maybe.

Christianity is widely practiced in Korea. However, this does not necessarily mean the inactivity of the traditional religions. South Korean cultural identity can be understood in terms of layers of religious thought that have been formed over 5,000 years. Each layer must be respected as a worldview that has survived in the spirituality of the Korean people, and the interaction of all the layers with one another must be analyzed in order to understand Korean culture. Having discussed Christianity in chapter 2, we turn our attention n the next two chapters to Shamanism, Buddhism, Confucianism, Taoism, Korean indigenous religions, and modernism as complementary and competing religious layers in Korean spiritual identity. In chapter 5 we discuss how there may be an emerging convergence of ideas among these layers that can provide guidance for the future of humankind.

Shamanism

Shamanism is the deepest layer of religion in Korea.[2] As the oldest religion in Korea, it has had a significant impact on forming Korean culture.

Shamanism is distinguished by the practices of seeking to solve human problems through a meeting of humanity and the spirits. *Mugyo*, Korean Shamanism, is "a method that human beings can use to interact with any god or spirit—not just those found in animism, but also deceased ancestors or deified heroes from the past, for example. Shamans become channels for human beings to contact a wide variety of invisible personalities."[3] There are three elements—deities, shaman and client—that compose a *gut*, the religious ceremony led by a *mudang*.

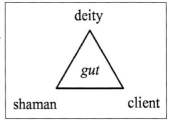

> A charismatic shaman in Korea goes into a trance in order to be possessed by a spirit and then lets that spirit speak through her to members of her audience. Through her, Koreans are able to plead with spirits to stop afflicting them with physical, financial, or personal problems, or are able to talk once again with recently deceased loves ones . . . People go to shamans seeking solutions to practical problems, such as family financial woes, worry over a daughter's marriage prospects, or a son's chances of getting into a good unviersity, or health problems within the family.[4]

Shamanism has survived for centuries in spite of periodic persecution and oppression. Confucian scholars and politicians, especially, could not leave Shamanism alone. Shamans, to the eyes of Confucianists, were misleading people by summoning wicked spirits and ghosts.[5] Therefore, Shamanism was suppressed by the Joseon dynasty. The fate of Shamanism was again at risk during the Japanese occupation. During the colonial rule, the Japanese tried to eradicate everything related to Korean traditional culture. After the Independence in 1948 Shamanism was persecuted by Christians. President ChungHee Park made Shamanism a target of suppression because his modernization policy demanded following Western culture; therefore,

2. Choi, *Understanding Koreans and Their Culture*, 217.

3. Baker, *Korean Spirituality*, 20.

4. Ibid., 21.

5. Choi, *Understanding Koreans and Their Culture*, 220.

the traditional village religious rituals represented by Shamanism were the first thing to be eliminated. The results were devastating. The government not only drove the *mudangs* into hiding, but wiped out many local shrines.[6] As a result, during the 1970s the number of shamans and clients shrank. However, the policy of persecution reversed in the 1980s, and since then there has been a gradual increase of practitioners of Shamanism.[7]

The future of Shamanism itself seemed uncertain in the late twentieth century. Observers believed that many of the functions in the future probably would be performed by the psychiatric profession as the government expanded mental health treatment facilities. However, experts have been surprised by the resilience of shamanistic beliefs and practices. Many Koreans love to consult with fortunetellers; estimated by some to be in the tens of thousands.[8] "The only element of Korea's folk religion that remains strong and viable in the twenty-first century is Shamanism . . . Koreans who seek supernatural help and who want to do so via intermediaries from the folk tradition can still hire a shaman."[9]

Since Shamanism has been rejected and its practitioners persecuted for hundreds of years, how does one explain the fact that South Korea has one the most active shamanistic practices of any modernized country in the world?

In some ways this is a Western-type question that ignores the persistence of Shamanism in the United States and other Western countries. Zora Neale Hurston[10] and Karen McCarthy Brown[11] conducted anthropological studies with shamans practicing in the United States. Bob Marley, a practitioner of the Rastafarian movement, has been popular among United States young people. When I (James Poling) was a pastor, there were practices of German hoodoo and hexes practiced by members of my German American congregation. Wicca and other pre- and post-Christian practices have experienced a revival in the United States in the last fifty years. These practices are evidence of the persistence of shamanistic beliefs even in a

---

6. Ibid., 221

7. Choi, *Folk-Religion*, 17.

8. Choi, *Understanding Koreans and Their Culture*, 174.

9. Baker, *Korean Spirituality*. 25.

10. Hurston, *Tell My Horse*. Zora Neale Hurston (1891–1960) did anthropological studies of folkways in the southern United States and the Caribbean and published many studies and novels: *Dust Tracks on a Road*; *Their Eyes Were Watching God*; *Jonah's Gourd Vine*; *Moses, Man of the Mountain*; *Mules and Men*; and *Every Tongue Got to Confess*.

11. Brown, *Mama Lola*.

culture like the United States, where such practices are often thought to have been virtually eliminated.

In addition to being a religious practice, Shamanism is part of the intense interest in South Korean "cultural nationalism." Starting with the Donghak religious movement of the late nineteenth century, religious leaders, artists, and scholars have been asking whether there is an essence of Korean spirituality, and, if so, how it will survive the onslaught of modernism. The most recent expression is large public interest in traditional Korean art, architecture, music, and religion. Just as Europe spent large amounts of its wealth to restore its cathedrals and other historical buildings after World War II, so Korea has invested precious wealth in restoration of Buddhist temples all over Korea, Silla palaces in Gyeongju, and the Joseon palaces in Seoul. In addition, many young people study traditional Korean arts and music. Nearly every university has an orchestra that plays traditional Korean music using traditional instruments.

The meaning of cultural nationalism as a social movement is contested. Some say that the search for an authentic Korean identity and spirituality originated in the nineteenth century in order to deal with the crisis of that time, and that much of the history of Korean spirituality and culture has been exaggerated and romanticized. Some think that the current motive for this recovery is the crisis brought by modernism itself as traditional family and community life is increasingly disappearing. Undoubtedly there are traditions or art, music, and ritual that predate the invention of writing and ideas of modern historiography. The public demand for the recovery of Korean spiritual identity is unabated.

Cultural nationalism is a social movement that functions both as a retrieval of historical traditions and a construction of new ideologies. The retrieval of beliefs and practices enabled people and cultures to survive over many centuries, and they should not be lost. But the movement is also a new ideological construction for political purposes. For example, belief in authentic Korean spirituality helped to fuel resistance to Japanese colonialism, while the Japanese government was imposing its own invention of the cultural past to legitimize its empire. More recently cultural nationalism was important for the democracy movement that opposed tyrannical Korean government policies. Modernism requires new identities that never before existed in history, but the people also need a sense of continuity with past traditions. How to balance both sides of this contradiction is a challenge for every group that wants to be a people.[12]

Many South Koreans believe that spirits are real forces in the world who need to be consulted for important decisions and for times of crisis. In Korea, shamans become psychic counselors. A *mudang* may carry out several important functions; among them the role of "counselor" may deserve special attention in the field of pastoral care.[13] Shamans survive because people believe they need them. When Koreans are faced with troubles that are difficult to bear, they seek advice from shamans. "Shamans are mediators who connect people with spirits and seek harmony between the two entities by soothing people's wounded hearts."[14]

Korea has imported many religions from outside: Buddhism, Confucianism, and Christianity. The religion of the ancient period did not disappear when other religions came. Rather, Shamanism became the substratum of all Korean religious experience and has shaped the development of all religions and philosophies that have been transmitted to Korea, including Buddhism, Confucianism, and Christianity.[15] Each religion takes its root in the mind of Korean people by way of exchanging elements with *Mugyo*.

Many shamanistic elements can be still found in Buddhism. In almost every Buddhist temple in Korea, there is a separate shrine building for

12. The Nazi use of *Volk* as a rationalization for national terror was in the air during the same time that some Korean politicians were invoking the Korean *minjok*. "*Minjok* and *minjung* derived from Chinese. While the original meaning of 'jok' in minjok was 'tribe' sharing a common ancestor, 'jok' is now more generally used to designate a race, or ethnic group, e.g. 'mong-jok,' meaning Mongolian race. When 'jok' is combined with 'min' (people), as in 'minjok,' the word becomes loaded with a heavily racial character. It refers to the Korean 'nation,' but puts a strong emphasis on the Korean people's sharing of common blood and a common ancestor, Tan'gun. It is an emotionally loaded term which has been used with great effect to call for the Korean people's absolute and unconditional love and loyalty for the nation. '*Minjung*,' is a combination of 'min' (people) and 'jung' (mass) . . . The students worked hard at shifting the discourse about the nation from minjok to minjung (the masses) in the context of democratizing Korea. This transformation challenged Koreans' view of their country's 'mass of ordinary people.' The term '*minjung*' was associated with dissatisfied crowds of common people as early as the Tonghak peasants rebellions in the late nineteenth century. The later meaning of minjung was profoundly re-shaped by the 1980s student movements which added a socialist character to the image of the nationalistic and righteous minjung. I am grateful to Chol W. Kim, my father-in-law, Korean translator and linguist, for clarifying the etymologies of these two key concepts" (Walhain, "Minjok," 85–86).

13. Choi, *Folk-Religion*, 61.

14. Choi, *Understanding Koreans and Their Culture*, 224.

15. Grayson, *Korea: A Religious History*, 270.

shamanic deities: the Samseonggak (Mountain Spirit) and Chilseong-shin (Spirits of Great Dipper).[16] Shamanistic beliefs and practices can be seen in Christianity as well. For example, in Western churches, prayer meetings at dawn are rare occasions; but in Korean churches they have become almost a daily practice, as it is both in *Mugyo* and in Buddhism. We can also observe the *sangido* (mountain prayer) customs, faithfully practiced by some Protestant ministers, popular among both preachers and the faithful.[17] One might even say that the Pentecostal "prosperity gospel" is an appropriation of shamanistic promises of blessings from benevolent spirits.

> In the early days of Protestant propagation, many church missionaries and their followers identified *mugyo* as their prime target to eradicate. But history shows everything has worked out the other way around. Contrary to their wish to destroy local Shamanic elements or at least weaken their influence, the evangelists found Korean Shamanism a fertile soil in which to cultivate their faith. Indeed, the church has flourished because it, in spite of itself, has accommodated many Shamanic elements into its system of belief. Church authorities would hesitate to agree, to be sure. But underlying the spectacular success Korean churches have achieved in modern times, there are local Shamanic elements that have made substantial contributions, it should not be forgotten.[18]

Shamanism has existed as the basis and at the root of Korean minds. In understanding Korean culture and spirituality in depth, Shamanism and *gut* are significant resources. Shamanism needs to be respected as part of Korean history and culture. "From Shamanistic traditions, [Koreans] have learned about this-worldly nature of being and its physical immediateness."[19]

Buddhism

"With the advent of Buddhism in the Three Kingdoms' era, Korea women's consciousness of space and time went through a great leap. They could develop a more extended nationalistic view, and with the conception of 'nothingness' or 'void,' they could have more control over this-worldly disasters and restrictions. They could also get the perceptions of 'nirvana'

16. Choi, *Folk-Religion*, 49.

17. Ibid., 51.

18. Ibid., 54.

19. Lee, "Study of Korean Women's Spirituality," 5.

or of 'causality' and the sharp awareness of the sacred and the profane in relation to human sexuality."[20]

Two major streams of Buddhism exist in practice. The meditative form focuses on enlightenment with "its promise of effective techniques for escaping suffering by developing insight that will dissolve the illusions that cause that suffering."[21] The compassionate form focuses on offering prayers and gifts to gods for solving practical problems of common people, thus providing "a font of supernatural power for coping with the problems of everyday life in this world . . . and assistance in overcoming intractable health, financial, or family problems."[22]

Buddhist temples serve as communities of fellowship and education. Children and youth groups are organized for various activities and adults gather together to study and serve the needs of others in charity work. "When Buddhism entered Korea in the late fourth century, it initially took the guise of the more powerful form of folk religion. Korea's first Buddhist monks performed miracles that suggested that the Buddha could heal diseases that the less powerful gods of folk religion could not."[23]

In the early years, Buddhism coexisted with Shamanism due to the peaceful nature of Buddhism. However, once Confucianism became the state religion in the fourteenth century, Buddhism and Shamanism suffered oppression from the government, which lasted for several hundred years. As a result, the Buddhist monks became among the lowest class in the society. "During the Joseon period, the number of Buddhist monasteries dropped from several hundred to a mere thirty-six. The royal court placed limits on the number of clergy, land area, and ages for entering the sangha. The final restrictions prohibited monks and nuns from entering the cities and Buddhist funerals and begging were outlawed."[24] For survival, Buddhism began to adopt some practices of Shamanism. Thus, the mountains that were believed to be the residence of spirits in pre-Buddhist times became the sites of Buddhist temples.

During the colonial period (1910–1945), the Japanese government tried to "Japanize" Korean Buddhism. By the end of colonial rule, the majority of Korean Buddhist priests, who were formally celibate, were married.

20. Ibid.
21. Ibid.
22. Ibid., 18–19
23. Baker, "Introduction," in Buswell, ed., *Religions of Korea in Practice.* 18
24. "Korean Buddhism."

This was the obvious influence of Japanese Buddhism in which celibate monks were still rare."[25] After independence in 1948, Korean Buddhism went through years of conflict and disintegration. The biggest obstacle was the struggle for power between the married monks and celibate monks and fights over the control of temples. As the conflicts continued, the influence of Buddhism decreased and Buddhism continued to lose followers to Christian missionaries, who were able to capitalize on these weaknesses. It is interesting to note that an important reformation in modern Korean Buddhism was the result of actions taken by the first president, Syngman Rhee (1875–1965), who was a Methodist. In 1954, during visits to Buddhist temples, he was shocked at the practice of clerical marriage which came from Japanese colonialism. Rhee initiated a national movement for the purification of clerical Buddhism. The result was the continuation of the Jogye-jong as a celibate order and the creation of the Taego-jong as an order of married clergy. These two orders constitute the two largest branches of Buddhism in contemporary Korea. The head temple of the Jogye-jong is the Jogye-sa, and the head temple of the Taego-jong is Bongwon-sa, located near Yonsei University in western Seoul.[26]

During the late twentieth century, Korean Buddhism made an effort toward reformation and has experienced a resurgence of commitment and energy. A visitor to South Korea can see the fervent devotion of many people by visiting the important Buddhist temples. Especially on holidays, thousands of people come to pray, drink from the pure springs, attend public rituals, and study with the monks.

A traveler to the mountains in Korea will be amazed at the many temples. If Confucianism was relatively indifferent to making physical artifacts, Buddhism created many highly artistic temples and other buildings. Therefore, among all cultural artifacts in Korea, 70 to 80 percent are related to Buddhism due to its long history in Korea.[27] Many are famous: Seoguram Grotto, Bulguk Temple, Emile Bell, etc. Buddhism is a Korean religion which has constructed and contributed to Korean tangible cultural assets.

25. Choi, *Understanding Koreans and Their Culture*, 214.

26. Grayson, *Korea: A Religious History*, 230–31.

27. Choi, *Understanding Koreans and Their Culture*, 205.

Taoism

If a young Korean were asked to name three religions that have influenced Korean spirituality, he or she would name Confucianism, Buddhism, and Taoism. That is what Korean people have learned at school. "The term *Dao* means a road, and is often translated as 'the Way' . . . Dao is the process of reality itself, the way things come together, while still transforming. All this reflects the deep seated Chinese belief that change is the most basic character of things. In the *Yi jing* (Classic [Book] *of Change*), the patterns of this change are symbolized by figures standing for sixty-four relations of correlative forces and known as the hexagrams. Dao is the alteration of these forces, most often simply stated as yin and yang."[28]

The image of the ideal person resembles a newborn infant, who lives naturally and free from desires. The ideal person releases yin and embraces yang, blends internal energies and thereby attains harmony. The ideal person is like water and embodies Tao in practice and creates peace. Over hundreds of years, the Taoist concepts like yin/yang, naturalness, oneness with nature, living according to nature are deeply embedded in Korean spirituality.

The Tai symbol represents a time of great fortune, success, and peace because heaven and earth unite. Such principles of yin and yang in which opposing forces belong together in harmony are basic to Korean culture. The Taegeukgi, or South Korean flag contains the symbol of the Tao (yin and yang surrounded by symbols from the *Yi Jing*).[29] It was officially adopted by the South Korean government in 1949.

Taoism as a religion has many temples and monks in Asia, all of them pursuing human immortality. Do Koreans really know this Taoism? No. Then why do Koreans think Taoism is one of the major religions? Religious studies scholar JoonSik Choi analyzes this as the result of a Chinese-centered perspective toward Korean history and spirituality. Even though Koreans are familiar with some concepts of Taoist tradition—such as the Taoist hermit, the Jade Emperor, Taoist fairy, Feungsu Theory—there are few if any Taoist temples or Taoist monks (*dosa*) in Korea.

What has been familiar to Koreans is not a religious but philosophical Taoism, in other words, "what Laozi and Zhuangzi taught."

---

28. Littlejohn, "Daoist Philosophy."
29. Wilhelm and Baynes, *The I Ching.*

> *Wu wei* is a difficult notion to translate into English. Yet, it is generally agreed that the traditional rendering of it as "nonaction" or "no action" is incorrect. Those who *wu wei* do act. Taoism is not a philosophy of "doing nothing." *Wu wei* means something like "act naturally," "effortless action," or "non-willful action." The point is that there is no need for human tampering with the flow of reality. *Wu wei* should be our way of life, because the Tao always benefits, it does not harm . . . The expressions of the movement of Tao are not opposites, mutually excluding and including each other. They represent the ebb and flow of the forces of reality: yin/yang; male/ female; excess/defect; leading/following; active/passive. As one approaches the fullness of yin, yang begins to horizon and emerge.[30]

One influence of Taoism as a religion can be seen in *Kigong* meditation and *Kuksundo* abdomen breathing exercise. Some new religions such as *Chondogyo* and the *Jeungsan* traditions appropriate and blend Taoist practices into their communities. Choi thinks that Koreans have not needed Taoism and Taoist monks because shamans have been practicing similar religious funcations already.[31]

Confucianism

Confuscianism developed from the teachings of the Chinese philosopher Confucius from the sixth century BCE. Confucianism teaches that human beings are teachable and improvable through personal and communal efforts called self-cultivation. A main goal of Confucianism is the nurturing of virtue and the development of moral perfection. The term *junzi* is crucial to classical Confucianism. "The *junzi* is the person who always manifests the quality of *ren (jen)* in his person and the displays the quality of *yi (i)* in his actions (4.5)."[32] The gentleman is one who has a virtue of *ren*, (humanity or benevolence) and *yi* (righteousness) . . . It is through *li* (ritual) that people cultivate *ren* and *yi*. *Li* can be seen in the many rules, manners and rituals Koreans have developed through the influence of Confucianism.

While Buddhism provided many tangible artifacts in Korea, the legacy of Confucianism remains a fundamental part of Korean society in a different way. Confucianism influenced Korea by shaping the moral system,

---

30. Littlejohn, "Laozi (Lao-tzu, fl. 6th C. BCE)."

31. Choi, *Hankuk Jonggyosa Baro Bogi*, 63.

32. Richey, "Confucianism."

ways of communication, proper manners, and social relations between generations, gender, and social classes, and providing the basis for much of the legal system.

The reality of Confucian influence is apparent to any United States visitor to Korea. The hospitality of Koreans is often confusing for those who have never experienced such generosity. There are rituals of respect between teachers and students, older and younger persons which can be confusing. It seems apparent that these customs and rituals are written deeply on the Korean psyche and do not change quickly.

One of the puzzles of Confucianism is that it does not function as a religious organization with temples, clergy, and religious activities. Less than one percent of South Koreans identify themselves as Confucians when asked about their religion. Half of all South Koreans deny that they have any religion at all. How does Confucianism survive without any of the outward signs that it is a religion?

Rather than organizing itself into a typical religion, Confucianism took a different path. First, it organized educational institutions: schools of esteemed scholars and universities. Confucius was one of the greatest educators. He insisted that in education there should be no class distinctions. He believed that learning was not only for gaining the skills for jobs, but for growth in moral judgment and self-realization. The contemporary Korean obsession with education may be a legacy of Confucius.

Second, Confucianism organized itself around government service. Confucius established a system for training in administrative and diplomatic arts. The system was later adapted as a central government examination system in selecting senior officers. The Joseon dynasty used Neo-Confucianism to design education and testing procedures for various administrative posts needed by the monarchy. The effect of this organization was the ideal of raising the quality of bureaucratic organization at every level and opening opportunities for social status based on merit rather than the feudal caste system.

Third, Confucianism developed rituals and values for families and local villages. It is quite well known that *ren*, the Confucian version of love, is the highest virtue. How is it different from Christian love or Buddhist compassion? What are the attributes of *ren* and how do Koreans practice it? Compared with other world religions, the uniqueness of Confucianism lies in the fact that its teachings always begin with the family.[33] In fact, family is

---

33. Choi, *Understanding Koreans,* 18.

its main pillar. Among the many religions worldwide, Confucianism is the religion that most strongly emphasizes the patriarchal family.

Confucianism has encouraged strong ties of loyalty and filial piety in five basic relationships: father/son, older brother/younger brother, husband/wife, king/subject, and friend/friend.[34] All of these principles became deeply embedded in Korean society.

From this legacy of Neo-Confucianism came an ideology of strict gender differences and distinct gender roles. It creates conflict with modern social ideas of gender equality.[35] In the late nineteenth century, many women, especially in educated classes, were restricted to the home and denied opportunities for public life. Everyday existence for women among the common people was extremely harsh because they had to work in the field and manage the home. The five relationships, emphasizing the hierarchy, dictated that women were to be obedient to their fathers when single, to their husbands when married, and to their oldest son when widowed. This strict patriarchal attitude continues in many forms into modern Korea.

Namsoon Kang is one of the feminist voices challenging Confucian patriarchy in Korea. "Feminists have exposed the oppressive potential of the resurgence of Confucian familism."[36] Kang argues that the Confucian family is a patriarchal family in which religious piety and social structure are carried from father to son and in which women have no place. "The teaching of filiality is mainly focused on the relationships between fathers and sons. Since the family lineage is patrilineal, the family of the wife is excluded from the family lineage. This aspect is the most significant flaw in Confucian notion and practice of familism."[37] Kang suggests that the virtue of individual human rights and gender equality from Christianity provides a necessary corrective to Confucianism, and this idea gives hope for feminist values of a new society. "When Asians try to utilize resources from Asian traditions, the consequence of these efforts should be to enhance the quality of our lives. If the traditions cannot provide better lives that contemporary women aspire for, women should make use of other cultural and religious traditions and learn from them."[38] Kang is pessimistic that ideas of gender justice are compatible with Confucianism.

---

34. Baker, *Korean Spirituality*, 42.

35. Baker, "Introduction," in Buswell, *Religions of Korea in Practice*, 21.

36. Kang, "Confucian Familism, 168.

37. Ibid., 174.

38. Ibid., 185–86.

In contrast to the arguments that Kang makes, EunSun Lee acknowl-
edges the legacy of patriarchy in Korea, but suggests that Confucianism is
only partly responsible: "Korean feminists criticize [Confucianism] to be
most responsible for today's unjust condition of women, and they say that
throughout Korean history, women's status became worse, and particularly during the last Chosun period, their condition became dramatically
poorer . . . It seems to me unjust to interpret Confucian tradition in that
manner from the viewpont of sexual inequality only."[39] EunSun Lee then
tries to retrieve certain religious ideas from Confucianism that can support
gender equality and end the oppression of women.

> Confucian learning [is a way] to ritualize the whole process of
> life, from early morning till night and from birth till the time after
> death. It recognizes all of life as the way of sagehood. So, if Con-
> fucianism also learns from modern feminism that the patriarchal
> time has passed away in humankind's history, and if it abandons
> its traditional sexual application of its principle, it can provide us
> with good meaning and occasion to practice our body and mind
> harmoniously toward the way of sagehood. The real religiosity of
> Korean Confucianism is the humanization and ritualization of all
> of life.[40]

Given the enormous consequences of gender oppression over centuries in both East and West, and given the persistence of patriarchy in
modern societies, the feminist movement will continue the vigorous debate
about the role of Confucianism in constructing equality and justice in the
postmodern world. The debates about the relative contributions of Confucianism and Christianity to gender justice are important conversations in
Korea today.[41]

In the next chapter, we explore the development and influence of the
"new Korean religions" and modernism in the form of religion.

39. Lee, "Study of Korean Women's Spirituality," 6.

40. Ibid., 11.

41. "Our working assumption is that there is not one but many Confucianisms. All
made an indelible impact on women's lives." Ko, et al., *Women and Confucian Cultures in
Premodern China, Korea, and Japan*, 3.

4

Modern Korean Religions

WHEN THE PROTESTANT CHRISTIAN missionaries arrived from the United States in 1884, there was already a one-hundred-year-old debate about the future of Korean culture and religion. In the eighteenth century the Silhak intellectuals had studied Jesuit documents describing modern European ideas about human rights and practical solutions to human problems. Some scholars converted and started practicing the Roman Catholic faith. Because these adherents challenged some sacred practices such as the Confucian ancestor rites, they were brutally oppressed. By the end of the nineteenth century, Korean resistance to modernism was waning and the Joseon government was increasingly corrupt. The power of modern ideas combined with military and economic pressure from expanding Western empires created a crisis for Korea. One result of that crisis was the emergence of new Korean religions with the express purpose of combining the ideas of modernity with traditional Korean religions. In this chapter we explore three of these new religion, the emergence of Kimilsungism, and some of the influences of modernism itself as it functioned as an imported religious vision.

New Korean Religions

"It is estimated that there are more than two hundred new religions in South Korea today . . . [including] Chʼondogyo, Wonbulgyo (Won Buddhism), Taejonggyo, Tan (Dahn) World, Chungsando (Jeungsando), Taeson Chili-hoe (Daesun Jirihoe), and the Unification Church."[1]

1. Baker, in Buswell, ed., *Religions of Korea in Practice*, 28–29.

The new religions share certain common features. First, these religions recognized the devastated conditions of late nineteenth and early twentieth centuries and tried to bring a change through the idea of a new creation of heaven and earth. For example, Chondogyo stresses the aspect of changing; Jeungsando emphasizes relieving collective *han* through envisioning a new world; while Won Buddhism accentuates spiritual enlightenment. They are concerned with relieving the suffering of the masses and looked toward a utopian condition in this world. Second, they are syncretic religions which mixed together Buddhism, Taoism, Confucianism, Shamanism and Christianity to create a new system of belief. Third, these new religions display a strong element of nationalism in their doctrines and methods of propagation.[2]

In this section we briefly highlight three Korean new religions: Chondogyo (Donghak), Jeungsangyo (especially Daesunjinrihoe), and Won Buddhism.

The Chondogyo Tradition

Chondogyo (the original name was Donghak) is a new religion founded by JeWu Choi on April 5, 1860. *Chondo* means the "Heavenly Way," a way to the truth. JeWu Choi declared that everyone had *Hanullim* (God) in himself or herself. The followers of Chondogyo believe in *Hanullim*, who is within us. We should serve *Hanullim* within us (*SiCheonju*), because *Hanullim* and human beings are identical (*Innaecheon*).[3] This idea embraces the dignity of human beings. Since all human beings have *Hanullim* in themselves, they should be served as *Hanullim* is served without discriminating against age, social status, race, or gender. The ideal human being is the one who has *Hanullim* inside and is united with *Hanullim*. Human beings should achieve

---

2. Grayson, *Korea: A Religious History*, 240–41; Yang, "History, Basic Beliefs," 73–74.

3. Compare *Hanullim* to the Protestant name for God in Korean, *Hananim*. According to Don Baker, "Koreans had no indigenous term for God in the monotheistic sense until Protestant Christians began using the terms Hananim and Han˘ulim near the end of the nineteenth century. The fact that new religions such as Chŏndo-kyo and Taejong-kyo have had to coin their own names for God, Hanullim and Hanŏllim respectively, is cited as further evidence that there were no indigenous Korean terms for God until fairly recently. The author concludes that an indigenous Korean monotheism is an invented tradition" (Baker, "Hananim, Hanøunim," 105).

self-fulfillment, and try to seek a heavenly mind to be united with heaven through the cultivation of sincerity, reverence, and faith.[4]

Since Chondogyo thinks of the cosmos as one spirit, death means returning to the original one spirit. Chondogyo places more emphasis on present day life than on life after death. To build a kingdom of *Hanullim* is the goal of the religious life of followers. Believers of Chondogyo follow certain religious disciplines such as: 1) a twenty-one-character incantation; 2) a prayer ritual with a bowl of pure water, which symbolizes the source of life: harmony, freedom, equality, and peace; 3) Sunday services; 4) an offering ritual rice and prayers.[5]

Chondogyo has contributed to Korean history by being active in various political movements such as the Donghak rebellion in 1894 and the Korean Declaration of Independence from Japan in 1919. It is noteworthy that of the 33 signatories of the Declaration of Independence in 1919, 15 were members of Chondogyo.[6]

The Jeungsan Tradition

Jeungsangyo believes that its founder Juengsan Kang (1871–1909) was actually God the Almighty incarnated in human form. Although Jeung-sangyo splintered into various branches after Kang's death, two of them (Daesunjinrihoe, promoted by Hangyong Pak, 1917–1996, as a splin-ter of the branch Taegukto, which had been founded by Ch'olche Cho, 1895–1958, after he had a vision of Kang in 1917; and Jeungsando, which claims a lineage reaching back to Kang's family) each claim a membership in excess of six million.[7]

Daesunjinrihoe stresses "resolving grudges and helping others."[8] Wor-ship consists of prayers and food sacrifice to the Most Holy God held in services on Sunday morning and lasting several hours. Thousands of wor-shipers gather at the Yeoju Dojang and four other temples once a month for these services. In addition, believers visit the temples regularly, engage in education and prayers, and enjoy fellowship with one another. Each day

---

4. Im, "Origin, Core Ideas, and Faith of Cheondo-gyo," 38–39.

5. Ibid., 48–52.

6. Grayson, *Korea: A Religious History*, 238.

7. Baker, "Renewing Heaven and Earth," in Buswell, ed., *Religions of Korea in Practice*, 487–88.

8. "Symbol Mark of Daesunjinrihoe."

thirty-six believers are chosen to chant the sacred scriptures in the most holy building and pray for peace and harmony in the world, an end to resentment, and altruism among all people.[9] According to the webpage of Daesunjinrihoe,

> The religious order of Daesunjinrihoe not only conducts its propagation, education, and cultivation as its internal activities, but also externally executes charitable works, social welfare service and educational work.
>
> - Charitable Works, Daesunjinrihoc is trying to help old people at rest homes, the unfortunate young children at orphanages and other alienated people.
>
> - Social Welfare Service, Environmental protection, Traffic order, Street cleansing, Community development, Help for farming villages, Protection for missing children, Feast in honor of the elders
>
> - Educational Works, School Foundation of Daejin which was established by Daesunjinrihoe in January 1984 governs Daejin University and six high schools.[10]

I (James Poling) am familiar with Daesunjinrihoe because I have a friend who is a scholar and practitioner of this religion. I have visited the Central Preaching Headquarters in Yeoju, Korea (Yeoju Bonbu Dojang) and a second temple at Daejin University in Pocheon, Korea (Pocheon Sudojang). While I have little knowledge of the internal realities of this religion, I can report on what I have heard and seen. The leaders I have talked with say that they hope their religion will harmonize all the religions of the world including Christianity. They explicitly honor the Korean ancient religions of Dangun, Shamanism, Buddhism, Confucianism, and Taoism because they have contributed to Korean religious identity. They believe that new religious truth will move from Korea to solve the many conflicts that are destroying the world today.

The two temples I (James Poling) have visited are traditional Korean-style buildings lavishly decorated and immaculately kept. So far, Daesunjinrihoe exists only in Korea and has not sent out missionaries like the Unification and Christian churches. Leaders told me that they hope to engage in missionary efforts in the future, but so far they have concentrated

---

9. This information comes from Dr. GyungWon Lee, professor of philosophy at Daejin University, Pocheon, Korea.

10. "Symbol Mark of Daesunjinrihoe."

their work in Korea. The competition among the many religious groups in South Korea is apparently intense, and I have heard complaints from Christian leaders specifically about *Daesunjinrihoe* and its methods of recruiting. Given the aggressiveness of some Christian missionaries, I am not sure whether the various groups imitate one another, or whether the recruitment methods of one's competitors always appear to be more ruthless than one's own. There are charges that Daesunjinrihoe is a cult that requires unhealthy forms of personal and financial sacrifice from its members.

Levinas says that the core of love is the ability to intimately engage with someone who is "Other" without violence or a need to reduce the Other to familiarity.[11] In visiting the temples of Daesunjinrihoe and talking with its leaders, I (James Poling) confess a feeling of vulnerability and insecurity that is beyond my understanding. I understand the search for a deeper spirituality caused by the crisis of modernity in late nineteenth century. I too feel frightened by the violence and conflict in the world during my lifetime. I feel a sense of urgency about war, terrorism, environmental disasters, and human suffering, and I can understand belief in an apocalyptic future as appropriate for our time. I fear for my grandchildren and whether they will have the spiritual resources to cope with the problems my generation has passed on to them. I wish I could have more confidence that my faith was a direct revelation from God that would save the world. I am both intrigued by Daesunjinrihoe and confused by its understanding of human religious life.

Won Buddhism

Attaining enlightenment in 1916, Jungbin Pak (1891–1943) had a vision of an essential unity in all of the Asian traditions and appropriated what seemed relevant from them all. However, he believed that his system was closest to Buddhism. He declared that his form of religion was Buddhism as practiced by the ordinary person, not just by monks. He taught his followers that they were not to worship the Buddha by reverencing images but by reverencing Buddha everywhere, because the Buddha nature is everywhere.[12] Followers believe that there are images of the Buddha all over the world and the Buddha is worshipped everywhere. The Buddha represented

---

11. Scott, "Emmanuel Levinas's *Totality and Infinity*."
12. Grayson, *Korea: A Religious History*, 251.

the ineffable reality behind all things could be symbolized by a circle, or *won*, thus the origin of the name—Won Buddhism.[13]

Won Buddhism distinguishes itself from other forms of Buddhism, and tries to bring improvement into the world. It requires followers to foster "the cultivation of the mind to be free from desires and attachments, the examination of the facts of existence to see which ones lead to happiness or suffering, and the correct choice of a moral course of action."[14] The temples of Won Buddhism are located in cities and function like a local Christian church with Sunday and Wednesday services. Won Buddhism tends to emphasize practice; it highlights the balance between gaining faith with external help and putting it into practice through one's own efforts; it values discipline in daily life.[15] Won Buddhism is considered a reformed Buddhism in that it embraces the original Buddha's teachings and attempts to make them relevant and suitable for contemporary society.

North Korean Juche as Religion

Some scholars argue that the political ideology of North Korea is turning into the most recent new Korean religion in North Korea.

> *Chuch'e* seems at first glance to be readily understandable. It means self-reliance and independence in politics, economics, defense, and ideology; it first emerged in 1955 as P'yongyang drew away from Moscow, and then . . . [from China] . . . *Chajusong* (self-reliance), *minjok tongnip* (national or ethnic independence), *charip kyongje* (independent economy)—all these terms were antonyms of *sadaejuui*, which means serving and relying upon foreign power, which had been the scourge of a people who naturally incline toward things Korean. Added up, these ideas were the common denominators of what all colonized peoples sought at mid-century: their basic dignity as human beings . . . [*Chuch'e*] is really untranslatable; the closer one gets to its meaning, the more the meaning slips away. For a foreigner its meaning recedes into a pool of everything that makes Koreans Korean, and therefore it is ultimately inaccessible to the non-Korean. *Chuch'e* is the opaque core of North Korean national solipsism.[16]

13. "What Is Won Buddhism?"

14. Grayson, *Korea: A Religious History*, 253.

15. Yang "History, Basic Beliefs," 87.

16. Cumings, *Korea's Place in the Sun*, 413–14. See also Shin, "The Sociopolitical

During my (James Poling's) visit to North Korea, our group received written instructions not to take pictures of, point to, or otherwise gesture toward any picture of Kim IlSung during our trip. Given the watchful eyes of our North Korean guides, we all complied with this request. Originally "Kimilsungism" was a political strategy to unify the country in light of hostility and an unresolved state of war with South Korea and the United States. One of North Korea's main requests in recent talks with the United States is that the United States should promise not to engage in a first military strike against North Korea. This request makes sense if one has an accurate picture of the history of the Korean peninsula. In the process of unifying North Korea, the veneration of Kim IlSung has become religious devotion with strict guidelines on obedience to his principles as implemented by the current government. How this new religion will develop remains to be seen. Currently, this ideology or religion cannot be accurately studied by scholars because North Korea is closed to outsiders.

In this brief summary of some of the new religions of Korea, we have provided a window into a world that many Westerners do not understand well. What can seem exotic and strange to Westerners makes sense when seen within the longer history of Korea and the accumulated trauma of disruption and violence of the last century. Creative forms of religious imagination are part of the Korean cultural landscape and the new Korean religions must be respected for what they are trying to achieve, even though the "otherness" of these forms cannot be reduced to the familiarity of Western logic.

Modernism as Religion

Modernism, like Confucianism, does not present itself as a religion, but rather as a social movement that includes democracy, capitalism, and individual human rights. However, it is labeled as a competing religion by many conservative Christians who attack modernity's secularism, humanism, and atheism as enemies of Christianity. South Korea has attracted the attention of scholars because it seems to defy the idea that religion and modernism are incompatible. South Korea seems to challenge the consensus that secularism has a kind of historical inevitability as the successor to religion. Europe is often held out as the primary example of secular modernism replacing the practice of traditional religion. Less than five

Organism," in Buswell, ed., *Religions of Korea in Practice*. 519–33.

percent of Europeans are active church members. Conventional Western sociology assumes that as people are educated, urbanized and become active citizens in democracy, they are likely to ignore or reject religious beliefs and practices. However, some scholars believe that Europe is a special case because of the historical development of magisterial religion, or religion fully identified with the state. Secular modernism became a source of individual and corporate identity as a critique of the tyrannical state. However, in countries with secular governments such as the United States and South Korea, being religious is a way to develop individual identity as a critique of the state.[17]

What effects have modern ideas and practices such as urbanization, democracy, capitalism, and technology had on Korean spirituality? South Korea has experienced radical changes in a short time. In 1905, most Koreans were rural, illiterate farmers living at subsistence level. After decades of traumatizing violence, death and social change, over eighty percent of South Koreans today live in megacities in high-rise apartments and work for wages. South Koreans have one of the highest rates of education, literacy, and technology in the world. On the one hand, South Korea is a miraculous success story of how a poor nation can rise to become an economic, knowledge, and technology powerhouse on the global level. South Koreans are characterized by hard work, intelligence, hospitality, and respect. They seem to have maintained a deep sense of their human value during a period of agonizing national trauma. At the same time, the country is showing many of the wrenching problems of every modern society—increased divorce, increased family violence, increased rates of suicide and mental illness. How shall we evaluate these changes?

If modernism is an ideology that functions as a religion, how shall we characterize it? Scholars debate these issues endlessly without resolution. Adam Smith said that capitalism has three moral principles: individual self-interest, competition, and supply and demand that function in relation to three spheres: land, labor, and capital (natural resources, human resources, money for investment). This differs from feudal societies in which religious and political leaders controlled land, labor, and capital through preordained social roles and threats of violence. Modernism represents the liberation of land, labor, and capital from artificial control by religious and elite restrictions so that workers, managers and investors can interact as individual actors. Laborers sell their services to capital investors who exploit natural

17. We summarize the argument of Davie, *Europe: The Exceptional Case.*

resources for profit. Adam Smith's research suggested that individual actors seeking self-interest would produce economic prosperity for the common good. A concentration of wealth was required in order to maximize the productivity of land and labor. The explosion of technology is an extension of capital as it seeks to generate more and more wealth. Wealth leads to the invention of technology, such as computers, which enhances the productivity of labor and extends the useful value of natural resources. These assumptions evolved into the ideology of free market capitalism[18] which has become the dominant global economic system, what John Cobb calls, "economism."[19] The free market has become a kind of religion that aims to reorganize every nation on earth and knit everything together into one economic system. The fact that some nations will suffer violence during this transition is considered a necessary evolution toward a better future.

South Korea is an example of a nation that has moved quickly from a premodern to a modern, capitalistic society. In the ideological world of modernism, North Korea represents the consequences of choosing another path. One of the dangers in the world, according to modernism, is that failed nations will obtain nuclear weapons and use them to destroy the world before free-market capitalism can bring its benefits to the total world population. The "war on terrorism," some argue, is necessary in order to manage "the axis of evil" during this time of transition. It is not hard to hear themes of sin and salvation of a religious vision in this story.

If modernism in the form of free market capitalism is a religion, what are its practices and rituals? After September 11, 2001,[20] United States President Bush asked citizens to go shopping. One of the perceived dangers in the 9/11 crisis was that United States consumers would withdraw in fear and refuse to play their role in the global economy, thus triggering a recession. Within this understanding, citizens are best behaved when they operate out of materialistic self-interest as consumers, and when they use their creativity as workers to be as productive as possible. Both of these traits can be seen in the South Korean population where hard work and high consumption have been paired to fuel the national economic engine. Certain Korean values, such as filial piety, humility, and hard work,

18. See Poling, *Render unto God* for an extended form of this argument.

19. Cobb, *The Earthist Challenge to Economism*.

20. On September 11, 2001, the World Trade Center was destroyed by two airplanes hijacked by Al-Qaeda. The symbolic effect of this destruction has become an identity crisis for the United States and modernism itself.

contribute to the success of capitalism. Scholars have done research on how the consumer economy functions and found the highly symbolic value of every part of family life—the condo they live in, the car they drive, the technology they use, and the products they buy. Scholars also discovered the ambiguity of these symbols and the tensions within families as they try to live conflicting visions.[21]

A controversial topic of debate in Christianity is the so-called prosperity gospel of some Christian Churches.[22] South Korea has eleven of the twelve largest Christian congregations in the world. The largest is the Yoido Full Gospel Church. "On 18 May, 1958, just after the Korean War, Yoido Full Gospel Church held its first worship service. Five Christians attended including Pastor David Yonggi Cho. They met at the foot of a mountain in Daijo-dong in Seoul. In spite of the indescribably difficult conditions in Korea. Pastor Cho depended on help and inspiration of the Holy Spirit and with positive and active faith he told his congregation—We can do it! We can achieve! Let's try! Eventually, Yoido Full Gospel Church grew to become the largest church in the world with over 763,000 members."[23]

Pastor Cho preaches the threefold blessing: "1) The Blessing of Spiritual Well-being; 2) The Blessing of Our General Well-being; 3) The Blessing to be in Health."[24] This is usually translated at a practical level into promise of eternal life in heaven, promise of material wealth in this life, and promise of physical health. Through sincere and loyal religious practices, believers can benefit from a growing, modern global economy and overcome the obstacles that prevent them from succeeding.

Scholars suggest that Cho's prosperity gospel matches the rise of free-market capitalism in South Korea because it emphasizes the blessings of health and wealth as signs of salvation from God. People come to church to receive God's blessings and believe that if they work hard and achieve more prosperity, they prove God's faithfulness in their lives. This development seems to validate Max Weber's "Protestant Ethic" in which he argued that certain beliefs of Calvinistic theology as filtered through Scotland (the home of Adam Smith) helped European and United States populations

---

21. Nelson, *Measured Excess*; Hart, *From Tradition to Consumption*.

22. Lausanne Theology Working Group, Africa Chapter, "Statement On Prosperity Teaching."

23. Yoido Full Gospel Church, "Yoido Full Gospel Church Story."

24. Yoido Full Gospel Church, "Overview of the Threefold Blessing."

adjust their identities toward becoming workers and consumers under capitalism.[25] The same process seems to be happening in South Korea.

However, a contradiction of the Prosperity Gospel is that not everyone who prays and works hard will prosper, and those who do not prosper do not seem to be obvious sinners who deserve their suffering. The issue of innocent suffering faces every religion that promises practical benefits for belief and sincere practice. Theologians have debated the interpretation of the book of Job for centuries, making questions of theodicy among the more lively debates within popular Christianity. Of course, the prosperity gospel is a kind of tautology—"if you prosper, you are blessed by God; if you are blessed by God, you will prosper." Once a believer accepts this logic, it is hard to change one's thinking without the whole belief structure collapsing. So without self-critical leadership, the prosperity gospel can be self-perpetuating. As some scholars have suggested, for some people, there is a real relationship between personal discipline, hard work, and success under capitalism. So such a gospel can work for some people.

As modernism becomes the dominant religion in Korea does Christianity function as a force to forge a partnership between religion and free-market capitalism? A related question is whether this partnership is a good thing for the Korean people and the world. Korea is unique because particular world religions and local religious movements still function as genuine beliefs and practices. Such diversity is possible because the history of religions in Korea can be divided into four broad periods, each dominated by a particular religious tradition. The era of Shamanism encompasses all Korean history from primordial times to the advent of Buddhism in the fourth century (CE). The second era, the period of Buddhist dominance, extended generally from the fourth to the fourteenth century. Most historical Buddhist art and temples come from this period. The third era, the period of Confucian dominance, witnessed a complete reversal of the positions of Buddhism and Confucianism, with the result that Korean culture for the next five hundred years was formed by Confucian concepts and values, almost to the exclusion of other traditions. The fourth era, the post-Confucian period, shows the decline of formal Confucian influence on society, the revival of Buddhism and the rapid growth of Christianity as a recent import.[26] "In premodern Korea, it was not at all unusual for

---

25. The term "Protestant ethic" was coined by Max Weber. See Weber, *The Protestant Ethic and the Spirit of Capitalism* (1905).

26. Grayson, *Korea: A Religious History*, 271.

the same person to patronize shamans, pray at Buddhist monasteries, and perform Confucian rituals. The average Korean was not expected to identify exclusively with one religious tradition. Catholics changed that. They defined themselves as Catholics and even had an initiation ceremony (baptism) that indicated they had joined a new religious community and had severed ties with all other religious traditions."[27]

JoonSik Choi identifies three turning points in Korean religious history: the importation of Buddhism, the establishment of Confucianism as a state religion, and the coming of Christianity. Korean people did not passively receive those foreign religions. Rather, they created Korean-style religious traditions out of their own creativity, culture, and spirituality.[28] As previously indicated, Shamanism formed the spiritual basis upon which all later religious traditions would be built.

How has Korean spirituality developed in the centrifuge of ancient and modern religious influences? We respond to this question in the next chapter.

27. Baker, "Introduction," in Buswell, ed., *Religions of Korea in Practice*, 26.
28. Choi, *Hankuk Jonggyosa Baro Bogi*, 8.

5

Is South Korea a Postmodern Culture?

As we have talked with religious leaders and studied the religious plural-ism of South Korea, we have heard versions of the following three state-ments.[1] We will use three statements as guides for the focus in this chapter on the religious identity of the South Korean people.

1. Christianity is saving Korean spirituality from the failures of Con-fucianism, Buddhism and Shamanism. Many Korean Christians believe that Christianity has liberated the Korean people from the oppressive religious culture of the nineteenth century and offered a new future for the nation.

2. Christianity is a danger to Korean spirituality because of its con-nections with modernism and its rejection of historic Korean re-ligions. Many South Koreans believe in the traditional religious belief and practices and reject Christianity as a Western ideology that has been imposed by Western powers.

3. A new religious vision is emerging in Korea that offers a promise of healing for the world religions in the context of modern global realities. Some Koreans believe that something new is under de-velopment that will draw on insights from various traditional religions and secularism and pave the way for new interreligious understandings of reality.[2]

1. A different version of the ideas in this chapter was published as Poling, "Is There a Korean Contribution to U.S. Pastoral Theology?"

2. These statements are meant to be rhetorical and are not representative of any schol-ar's serious interpretation of history. "There is a long history of using "Confucianism" as a shorthand for something less amenable to a simplistic narrative: Chinese civilization,

Postmodern philosophy is a way of thinking about the current problems in Western cultures. It takes its name from the criticism of modernism, which developed in the eighteenth century. The basic ideas of Western culture—free market capitalism, individual human rights and freedom, and democracy—are best summarized in the United States Declaration of Independence in 1776. "We hold these truths to be self-evident, that all men are created equal, that they are endowed by their Creator with certain unalienable Rights, that among these are Life, Liberty and the pursuit of Happiness." The postmodern criticism suggests the need for less emphasis on individual freedom and happiness and more attention to the development of communities and the common good. The debate itself, not surprisingly, is controversial. The issue for this chapter is whether Korea can integrate the Western influences of capitalism, individualism, and democracy with its Eastern values of social order and family and group orientation.[3]

Is Christianity Saving Korea?

Many Christians take the position that Christianity has been a liberating and empowering spirit for the people and nation of South Korea after the failures of Confucianism, Buddhism, and Shamanism. They partly base their view on the state of Korean society in the late nineteenth century. In their opinion, Korea was a hermit kingdom that was incapable of interacting with other nations, and the majority of its people lived in desperate conditions of poverty and ignorance. The innovations of Christian

---

secret of Asian economic success, or obstacle to modernization" (Ko, *Women and Confucian Cultures in Premodern China, Korea, and Japan*, 3).

3. The philosophy of postmodern criticism developed in response to the perceived limitations of modernism. Some scholars believe that postmodern philosophy developed as a necessary critique of the individualism, nonrelationality, and claims to universality of modernism. In contrast, postmodern philosophies emphasize community, mutual relationships, and respect for multiple understandings of reality as an alternative to modernism. However, the validity of postmodernism criticism is contested. Other scholars believe that the postmodern move is just an extension of the logic of individualism and nonrelationality. That is, modernism has within it the logic of individualism that moves toward fragmentation and lack of cohesive community. What could be more modern than a philosophy that emphasizes relativism, pluralism, and difference? In addition, modernism has obviously not spent its energy as a social movement. For longer discussions of modernism and postmodernism, see the following: Griffin, *Whitehead's Radically Different Postmodern Philosophy*; Grenz, *Primer on Postmodernism*; Caputo, *Deconstruction in a Nutshell*.

(Western, modern) education and health care made significant differences in the quality of life for many Korean people. Poor families and women who had few rights within Korean society received special attention from missionaries, and some people responded eagerly to new opportunities for knowledge and power. Christian missionaries brought resources that benefited for many people.

Some argue that Christianity benefited Korea by preparing the Korean people for the survival of the brutal Japanese oppression that came during the early twentieth century. Christian piety offered forms of faith and practice that enabled the people to survive the political and economic oppression, especially the Japanese attacks on the language, history, and ideas of the Korean people. Many Christians believe that South Korea's later prosperity and world-class contributions have been possible because of Christianity and its vision of the world. The desperate condition of North Korea validates this claim for some. North Korea is a regime that reaffirmed its traditional identity and isolated itself from the world in ways similar to Joseon Korea before the twentieth century. But North Korea has been unable to develop and provide for the basic needs of its people, and the cost of its survival has been tyranny and oppression of political freedom and human rights. For those who believe Christianity has been a positive influence, North Korea provides an example what happens when Christianity is rejected.

Is Christianity a Danger to Korean Spirituality?

A different interpretation of Korea is that Christianity has been a disaster and a vehicle for the fragmentation and violence typical of societies that embrace modernism. Christianity came in Korea during a time of internal and external vulnerability. The Joseon dynasty had become corrupt. Japanese military strength with the backing of the Western empires attacked and pressured Korea during this vulnerable time and eventually overpowered the small peninsula unable to defend itself against the onslaught of foreign power and technology. Treaties made under military threat with France, Britain, and the United States further weakened Korea. Christianity weakened the Korean spirit internally by alienating the people from their traditional values and rituals and pitting educated classes against working people, rich against poor. The people could mount no united defense against the Japanese conquerors. Some leaders of traditional Korean religions claim that Christianity is a foreign and barbaric system of ideas and practices that contributed to Korea's near destruction.

According to this account, the only reason the South Korean people survived the colonization by Japan and subsequent war and disruption is that they have a five-thousand-year history of traditions that could not be destroyed by one hundred years of oppression. Many Korean converts to Christianity are still Confucians and Buddhists at heart, and these deeper layers account for the true survival of the Korean people. The "cultural nationalism" of the late twentieth century was an expression of a Korean spirituality that survived the destructive effects of modernism and its religious form through Christianity. Other scholars point out that the phenomenal success of the country's growth and prosperity comes because of traditional cultural values: the willingness of individuals to sacrifice for the common good, the respect that Koreans have for education and the wisdom of elders, the discipline to work hard, and self-cultivation. Economic prosperity has come to Korea not because of its natural resources or geopolitical position but because of the indomitable spirit of its people. This spirit comes from centuries of practicing traditional Korean religions.

In this interpretation of the modern history of Korea, North Korea's failure as a nation comes because of modernity's intrusion. Two-thirds of Korean Christians lived in North Korea until 1945, after which they fled or were killed. For six decades, Christianity had already contributed to the disintegration of traditional Korean society. When the North Koreans adopted the Marxist-Leninist ideology from Europe, and Russia in particular, it imported modern beliefs just as South Korea imported ideas from the United States. In fact, the cold war between capitalism and Communism is itself a construction of modernity. Therefore, South Korea and North Korea represent the two faces of modernity—one side emphasizing fragmentation of community and an ethic of greed, the other side emphasizing collectivism and tyranny in a distorted form of nationalism. These two options together have divided and nearly destroyed Korean society.

The fragmentation of South Korea under Christianity and capitalism can be seen in the destruction of the traditional Korean family and rising rates of mental illness, suicide, alcoholism, and interpersonal violence. As families move from traditional villages based on trust and respect into high-rise apartments of anonymous and utilitarian relationships, the coherence of communities is destroyed and individuals are left to fend for themselves. Modern South Korea is marked by a history of political dictators, corrupt government, and monopolistic corporations. Extreme differences of wealth and poverty fragment society, and families are caught in an confusion of consumerism. One should grieve the endless trail of apartment buildings where villages used to exist and wonder how the spirits of the people survive.

From this interpretation, one can understand the resurgence of public interest in traditional Korean arts and religion. Returning to the ancient traditions of Korea and rejecting the modern imports of capitalism and Christianity is the hope for the future. As the growth of Christianity stalls, some take comfort that the people are returning to their roots and dedicating themselves to heal this split in their spirits.

Is Korea Developing a New Religious Vision?

Some religious leaders suggest a third option: that the changes in Korean spirituality of the twentieth and early twenty-first centuries are experiments that have the potential to go beyond the limitations of Christianity and the traditional Korean religions. Even though modernism has contributed important values such as democracy, human rights, and creative freedom, human and natural existence is threatened by current global crises of war, poverty, economic exploitation, and environmental danger. The world is in desperate need of new perspectives that incorporate traditional religions, and a new vision that is interreligious, communal, and creative. No doubt there is enormous creativity in Korean intellectual life, and people are exerting energy and discipline that are intriguing to Western scholars.

The newly emerging Korean religions would demonstrate that new spiritualities are developing. These groups are consciously retrieving beliefs and practices from traditional Korean religions, Christianity, and modernism. The status of the emergent Korean religions is hard to evaluate,[4] and we do not have enough knowledge about the new religions to understand these groups. Our objective here is to explore whether Korean spirituality has something to contribute to Christian pastoral care in the United States, a more limited question. Are specific beliefs, worldviews, and practices valuable for the development of pastoral care in the United States given the crisis of modernity?

---

4. One United States scholar who is taking this challenge of new Korean religion seriously is Baker, *Korean Spirituality*. See also Buswell and Lee, eds., *Christianity in Korea*.

The third statement about Korean spirituality, the one suggesting a new religious vision, is not about the triumph of Christianity. It is the open question of whether Christianity, in cooperation with traditional and emerging Korean religions, will foster the development of a new spirituality to help humanity survive the modern crisis. It is a hope for something new that is genuinely postmodern and postcolonial, something that liberates the human spirit toward a compassionate global community. In the rest of this chapter, we look at stories that might give clues to what is happening in Korea, and, in the final two chapters, we develop ideas that offer deeper insight into Korean contributions to the human spirit.

The possibility of a new spirituality appeals to us as practical theologians because it implies that alternative human possibilities are worked out in practice over long historical periods, not invented in the minds of great intellectuals. Perhaps Korea is a new Israel where something new is happening in ways that are analogous to Israel in the first century. We do not claim to know if this is true. What we want to explore is more modest: what contributions can Korean spirituality make to pastoral care and theology? The answers to this question depend on how Korean people are responding to the contradictions of their culture—some inherited from the past, and some introduced through the imposition of modernism. The following stories illustrate contradictions within modern Korea, while they also illustrate a deep compassion that the Korean people have for those who are vulnerable as they respond to these contradictions.

The distinctive mark of Korean spirituality could be the courage to face into internal contradictions while responding with compassion to the suffering and hope of all people. "Many Koreans seem to have such compassion by nature (maybe unconsciously learned from our historical experiences), or feel responsibility for them from our deepest sides of the minds. I think that this is the 'original grace' for Koreans. Many scholars believe that our salvation should be good news to those nations or people who suffer."[5]

---

5. HeeSung Chung, Professor of Pastoral Care, Ewha University, Seoul, Korea, personal correspondence.

Stories That Suggest an Emerging New Vision

Compassion for Immigrant Brides

Korea has perceived itself as an ethnically homogeneous population with similar values and understandings of human life. However, in recent years, as the country has become part of the global economy, there has been an increase in immigrant labor from the poor countries of Southeast Asia. Some studies estimate that five hundred thousand to one million foreign workers live in Korea.

Among these immigrants have been thousands of "immigrant brides," many of whom have moved to rural areas because of the shortage of women in these areas. "Young Korean women leave rural towns for the lights and high-paying jobs of the cities, while sons often remain to take over family farms. Financially independent women consider marriage an option rather than a must. To make matters worse, by 2012 in South Korea there will be 124 men for every one hundred women in the age group of 24 to 30—a result of rampant abortions of female fetuses in the 1980s. In time, men begin to look abroad for brides."[6]

Some Korean men, often in their thirties and forties, respond to aggressive advertising that brides are available. For a reasonable fee, a man can travel to one of the Southeast Asian countries, pick a possible wife from a lineup at a hotel, and then negotiate a contract. If the negotiations are successful, the man returns home, and as soon as the woman gets a visa, she comes to join him. "The number of brides who came to Korea through spousal migration reached thirty-three thousand in 2009 alone, accounting for 10 percent of total marriages. The majority of migrant brides are Chinese, followed by Vietnamese. Most of them are married to farmers or fishermen and one-third of them get divorced. The average marriage lasts 3.1 years."[7]

Given the system that creates these marriages and the persistence of patriarchy, it is not surprising that there are high rates of domestic violence and other problems in these relationships. Rural families are often traditional, and a daughter-in-law must adapt and submit to her husband's family, often by obeying her mother-in-law. When the new bride does not speak Korean or have any family or economic resources of her own, she is vulnerable.

6. Choe "Foreign Brides Challenge South Korean Prejudices."
7. Suk, "Matchmaking in Korea."

Modern globalized culture has greatly contributed to the problem of immigrant brides. Whether these women find resources for healing and developing a new life in Korea often depends on the generosity of the church and nongovernmental organizations. MinAe Song, PhD, a staff member of the Yonsei University Pastoral Counseling Center in Seoul, ministers to immigrant women who come to Korea from Vietnam and Thailand. Through her initiative I (James Poling) had lunch with a student from Thailand who was studying at Ewha University and trying to help some of the Thai women in Korea survive. Unfortunately, globalization encourages immigration of workers while the patriarchal culture of Korea makes immigrant women vulnerable. In response, some Christian Korean women engage in social services to help support these women and engage in a prophetic confrontation of their society. The newspapers and other media are full of the stories of suffering and hope of immigrant women because their presence raises so many contradictory issues for the Korean culture.

I (HeeSun Kim) worked with immigrant workers for four years. In Korea, my ministry was working with immigrant workers who came to my church's free medical clinic (Good Neighbor's Clinic) every first and third Sundays. Recognizing the harsh treatment by Korean employers toward immigrants who were mostly undocumented, Korean churches have organized care and support systems to help them. Through my ministry, I heard many stories of how their hopes and dreams were destroyed and distorted by oppressive working conditions, harsh treatment, and low salaries. At the beginning, the church offered them only medical services. In time the ministry expanded as more Koreans wanted to help the immigrants. One day I asked a worker, "Are you sick today?" He said he was not sick. I asked him then why he was there that day. He said, "I am here because this church is becoming the place where I can relax and hang out with people. I meet my friends [immigrant workers] here and I am making more friends [Korean volunteers]." I could read his complicated feelings toward Koreans. I realized that the workers were coming not only because they wanted the medical care, but also because they were desperate for a community where they felt welcomed and cared for. At the same time, I understood the man's contradictory feelings toward Koreans. For many immigrant workers, it is Koreans who hurt them; but at the same time, it is also Koreans who try to care and heal their wounds even just a bit—compared to their deep wounds. Therefore, immigrant workers hate Koreans and love them. From that experience, I know that both Koreans and immigrants have mixed and ambivalent feelings: Koreans (mistreatment vs. compassion and care toward immigrant workers) and immigrant workers (love and hate toward Koreans). This ability to confront the contradictions of modern global markets with compassion may be a mark of a new spirituality.

Compassion for the People of North Korea

A powerful experience for me (James Poling) in 2008 was a one-day trip to Kaesong in North Korea through of the generosity of a colleague, Professor HeeSung Chung of Ewha University. In recent years, before the latest tensions between North and South Korea, North Korea had opened two areas near the border for pilgrimages by South Koreans: Kaesong and Geumgangsan (Diamond) Mountain. Thousands of South Koreans made this journey. On my trip, many middle-aged adults were taking their parents across the thirty-eighth parallel, I assume to fulfill the parents' wish to return to the north from which they fled between 1945 and 1953. I have met many people whose families originally came from North Korea; sixty years later they do not know what happened to their families and friends. They have had no communication since leaving. There have been some well-publicized reunions of long-lost families, but most South Koreans have not been able to establish any communication with their families. I was touched as we watched the gentle conversations between the South Korean pilgrims and the North Korean guides and supervisors. More than fifty North Koreans accompanied five hundred South Koreans on the day we traveled, allowing opportunities for significant interaction.

It seems that South Koreans are willing to do almost anything to reunify the country, even after all the violence and hostility of sixty years. This statement is supported by certain statistics. The South Korean churches have raised millions of dollars for aid to North Korea.[8] The South Korean government provided four hundred thousand tons of food aid and 350,000 tons of fertilizer annually from 2002 to 2008, amounting to 30 percent of North Korea's food supply.[9] Former President DaeJung Kim received the

8. "South Korea offered Monday to ship 10,000 tons of corn to North Korea in what would be the first such government-financed aid in nearly two years. The offer is far smaller than what South Korea used to ship—500,000 tons of rice and 300,000 tons of chemical fertilizer—to help the North make up its yearly food shortages of up to a million tons" (Choe, "South Korea Offers Food Aid to North."). See also Haggard and Noland. *Famine in North Korea*; and Haggard and Noland, "Aid to North Korea," 797.

9. Lankov, "N. Korea faces Unprecedented Food Crisis since 1990s."

Nobel Peace Prize in 2000 for his "sunshine policy" toward North Korea. Essentially his policy was to act as benevolently as possible toward North Korea in order to create the possibility of communication and talks toward reunification. Kim's policy was controversial in Korea and in the United States. A significant part of the money sent to North Korea has gone to support the government rather than the people, and there is great uncertainty whether the relationship with North Korea will move toward peace and/or reunification. Continuing President Kim's policy of benevolence was not popular in Washington during the administration of President George W. Bush. When the current president of South Korea, MyungBak Lee, withheld funds from North Korea and joined President Bush in demanding faster progress in North Korea to stop the development of nuclear weapons, many South Korean people were upset.

President Lee is a Presbyterian elder who often supervised parking at the Somang Presbyterian Church. One of my (James Poling's) colleagues used to be a pastor in that congregation and knows President Lee to be a person of integrity and faith. Christians have long been active leaders in government and business, and at the same time, the churches have been actively sending development aid to North Korea. South Korea faces deep contradictions in its relationship with North Korea. Many South Korean Christians are politically conservative and anticommunist and reject any compromise with North Korea. At the same time they feel the power of the historical unity of language, culture, family, and religion and yearn for reconnection. What to do about the relationship with North Korea is a constant preoccupation. Can the South Korean people find the spiritual resources to respond with benevolence to North Korea and work toward reunification of the peninsula within the context of hostility that is the legacy of global politics?

President Lee and the Beef Crisis

At the end of my (James Poling's) visit in June, 2008, South Korea was experiencing street demonstrations involving hundreds of thousands of people. Dozens were injured and hospitalized and much property was destroyed. The legislature was forced to be in recess because many legislators were boycotting sessions in support the demonstrations. Because certain policies of President Lee were so unpopular, his entire cabinet submitted their resignations and many leaders were replaced. President Lee apologized to the Korean people for his insensitivity to their needs and desires. When President Lee was elected the tenth president of Korea on August 20, 2007, he won the largest popular support in the history of Korean democracy (since 1991). When he took office on February 25, 2008, his approval ratings dropped, and by May 2008 only 20 percent of the electorate supported his leadership. What happened?

The ostensible reason for the demonstrations was to protest resuming imports of United States beef as part of the United States–South Korea Free Trade agreement. Under this agreement, United States beef would be imported and sold in Korea, thus ending a three-year boycott of beef imports that began with the discovery of mad cow disease in the United States. But why would a disagreement over beef imports threaten the administration of a president just elected to a five-year term?

Reasons for the beef demonstrations:

1. Genuine concern over the safety of United States beef. Many Koreans believe that different standards are used for United States beef intended for domestic use and for beef intended for exportation. According to HahnShik Min, "Personally, I would agree to importing United States beef if the same safety standard is applied for both domestic [United States] and exported [to Korea] beef." Many Koreans believe that the United States dumps unsafe beef on the Korean market.

2. Opposition to the free-trade agreement. The people are suspicious of unfair negotiations between the small country of Korea (GDP $1.2 trillion) and the United States (GDP $13 trillion—a ratio of 10–1). Free trade is a misnomer because it increases trade for superpowers and increases vulnerability for emerging economies.

3. Traditional government protectionism of the Korean economic system. The government has protected rice farmers, beef farmers, and industries such as cars, steel, computer technology and telecommunications from foreign competition. Fragile smaller economies need boundaries so that they can increase local and regional self-sufficiency.

4. Health and Environmental concerns. Pollution of food, water, and air from the United States, China, Korea, and the like. The use of fertilizers and herbicides to grow food, overuse of hormones, animal feed, and unsafe feedlots create enormous environmental

problems. Modern scientific agricultural is dangerous for human beings and threatens natural wisdom from traditional cultures.

5. Unilateralism of President Lee's administration. The beef crisis was a convenient way for some politicians to oppose the current political party in power. Koreans are very sensitive to concentrations of power in the executive branch of government and are always on guard to protect democratic freedoms.

6. Anti-Americanism. There is a long history of tensions with the United States military presence, the unevenness of economic globalization, the austerity of the 1997 IMF crisis and economic restructuring, and even the Iraq war. President Lee met with President Bush at Camp David in 2008 and was criticized for being pro-American. The United States role in Korea has been ambiguous.

Leaders of global capitalism tend to see political demonstrations as a sign of instability, a deadly trait for a developing country. Investors do not like instability and the rapid global movement of money can easily punish a small country for acting too independently. Yet the Korean people have a long history of political protest and a long list of martyrs to show for it. One of the biggest demonstrations in recent years occurred on June 10, 2008, the anniversary of the death of HanYeol Lee, a student demonstrator from Yonsei University who was killed by a tear gas canister thrown by police officers in 1987.

The demonstrations in 2008 arose because Korea lives with deep contradictions between being a sovereign nation and being part of the global economy. While some commentators have criticized South Korea for its tolerance of immigrant brides, its complicated attitudes toward North Korea, and its politics that seem to border on anarchy, many Christians feel genuine compassion toward those caught in these unjust situations. Perhaps a deeper Korean spirituality enables the people to hold these contradictions together and work for a greater good.

Conclusion

In this chapter we have discussed insights related to contemporary Korea. These insights are tentative because Korea is an energetic and creative place that has captured the imagination of many people. We have tried to write down our impressions in a respectful way that can help create a bridge between United States Christians and Koreans. However, Korea is filled with contradictions that need to be addressed so that the people can have a healthy and prosperous future.

Thesis

Maybe new integration of traditional religions and modern ideologies that Korean spirituality brings into the global experience can inform other Christian churches.

This is a contestable thesis that helps us understand something I (James Poling) learned several years ago from a colleague, Jeffery Tribble.[10] Quoting one of his sources he said "The only thesis worth defending is one that is contestable. That is, whether a particular thesis is true depends on evidence, not just on language and logic." I realize that the content of Korea's contribution to United States churches is contestable, and in the right context, it would be vigorously contested. "A prominent characteristic of Korean religious and philosophical thought is its proclivity for sustained and open intellectual debate regarding fundamental principles—especially phenomenological issues that deal with the origins and manifestations of good and evil, soteriology, ethics, and so forth."[11]

One Korean pastor of a local church gives witness to the ambiguity of Korea's religious witness: "On the one hand, I have become pessimistic after all these years of division and conflicts between right and left, conservatives and liberals. Can Korean culture really find a way to be a postmodern community of mutual respect and relationship? Can the Korean church play a positive role in this process? On the other hand, whenever I encounter people with prophetic voices and genuine compassion, either inside the church or outside, my hope for a new community is rekindled. When I encounter foreigners who love Korea, not just our buildings, food, or scenery, but *real*

---

10. Jeffery Tribble, Professor of Ministry, Columbia Theological Seminary, Decatur, Georgia, USA. See also Booth, *The Craft of Research*, 95. They argue that strong claims must be a) substantive, b) contestable, and c) specific. Readers think a claim significant to the degree that it is contestable. It should lead them to think, "You'll have to explain that claim," because they have long thought otherwise, or because they never have thought about the claim at all.

11. Muller, "The Great Confucian-Buddhist Debate," in Buswell, *Religions of Korea in Practice*, 177

us, with our weaknesses and brokenness, I look at my country again with a new perspective."[12]

Everything in Korea is contested. That may be what makes Korea post-modern—any position a person takes is contestable and usually contested. Korea is developing a culture in which vigorous, emotional debate about just about everything is taking place. This creates a population deeply aware of the multiplicity and ambiguity of every human construction. If Korean culture can find a way to live as a community into such difference amidst a pluralism of religions and ideologies, perhaps it can show others the path.

"Everything in Korea is contested. That may be what makes Korea postmodern—every position one can take is contestable and usually contested." I (HeeSun Kim) really like this idea and appreciate that James Poling is able to see this part of Korea. For sure, there are many things that are contradictory and contestable. That is partly why it is hard to write a book about Korea: when Koreans try to talk about the concepts of *han* and *jeong* in English, we disagree with each other, saying, "That is not what *han* means or what *jeong* means." In addition, however, I suggest that there are some strong totalitarian tendencies in Korean culture that can be described as "collective madness." When a particular event happens, it sweeps the whole nation. There is almost no room for other voices to be heard. This characteristic of Korea does suffocate me sometimes. Fortunately, the passion of collectivism does not last long. Things can be forgotten quickly. Therefore, in my opinion, the statement "Everything in Korea is contested" can also be contested. And I hope it also might create potential for Korean spirituality. Korean spirituality cannot be grasped easily; it scoffs at our attempts to put it in order and tries to be slippery in order not to be categorized. Very postcolonial!

12. HahnShik Min, pastor, Korean Methodist Church, Seoul, personal correspondence.

6

Korean Contributions to Pastoral Theology

HAVING REVIEWED SOME OF the history, religion, and culture of Korean spirituality, we turn in the next two chapters to the opening question of this book—what are the implications of Korean spirituality for pastoral theology, care, and counseling? In chapter 6 James Poling, with critique by HeeSun Kim, summarizes several Korean concepts and correlates them with the Christian Trinity; in the final chapter, HeeSun Kim, with critique by James Poling, brings together a summary of the Trinity in Western theology along with several Korean concepts that address pastoral care issues of healing from domestic violence.

Values of Han, Jeong, and Salim

Creative Korean and Korean American theologians have identified three Korean concepts that express significant aspects of the spirit: *han, jeong, salim.* While these terms need to be understood within their context of culture and religion, we believe their meanings transcend the Korean situation.

Han

Han is perhaps the best-known Korean word in United States theology. It is often translated by the English word, "suffering." However, its meaning is much richer than the English word for "suffering." *Han* refers to the long-term, often intergenerational, effects of unrelieved trauma on persons, families, and communities.

Andrew Sung Park defines *han* as brokenheartedness—the wounded-ness of the heart. He states, "*Han* reverberates in the souls of survivors of the Holocaust, Palestinians in the occupied territories, victims of racial discrimination, battered wives, victims of child molestation, the unemployed and exploited workers."[1] *Han* is a wound of the heart, the sense of sadness, frustration, and anger that results when the human spirit is dominated and destroyed through evil systems.

Han is an ambiguous term because it can express itself in various directions. It can turn into righteous anger that demands justice for a wrong, or it can become rage that demands revenge and destruction to satisfy one's honor. *Han* can turn into depression, and even suicide as the self turns away from the world to seek escape and oblivion. *Han* can also develop into solidarity among those who have been unjustly treated, so that the sorrow of life is shared and anger at injustice leads to protest and political action. "In addition, *han* is the ability to be aware of the complexity of one's inner mind. *Han*-ridden people are those who are able to see the mixture of goodness and badness in themselves and others. There is no rigid cleavage between the goodness and badness of oneself and others, which can explain why *han*-ridden people are so depressed sometimes. Their enemies are also in themselves. There is no easy target within oneself or in others."[2]

After a century of war, violence, disruption, and fragmentation of Korean society and its effects on every family, *han* expresses the tragic reality of the Korean experience. Finding healing for *han* is one of the motives of the hundreds of Korean Christians who are studying pastoral counseling in Korea and the United States today.

The concept of *han* can help pastoral theologians understand the long-term consequences of trauma of various kinds: war, the oppression of poverty and deprivation, interpersonal and family violence, addictions, etc. The rich understandings of *han* express the reality of many persons who turn to pastors and trained pastoral counselors. During the complicated processes of healing from trauma, persons often feel a mixture of emotions: sadness, fear, rage, and revenge as well as determination to survive and a desire to collaborate with others to protect all vulnerable people who are threatened with violence.

---

1. Park, *Wounded Heart of God*, 10.
2. HeeSung Chung, personal correspondence.

Jeong

Jeong is often translated into English as "love," but *jeong* resists a simple English translation because it has many layers and richer meanings. *Jeong* has multiple faces. It is not easy to explain even in the Korean language. If you ask a Korean—what do you think *jeong* is?—each person will give you a different answer.

To begin simply, it means love and affection. When one person is regarded as having a lack of *jeong*, it means he/she is cold, not affectionate or compassionate enough. Many Koreans do not say goodbye at the door with their guest; they walk to the guest's car or at least walk with the guest a bit; otherwise the person or the relationship has no *jeong*. When Koreans share food with others, they give just a little bit more than the expected amount, even one spoonful more; otherwise, no *jeong*. In this sense, *jeong* means love and affection.

But to go further, *jeong* means longtime attachment or bonding with other persons with all the ambiguities of such relationships. People become close because of shared experiences over time, and *jeong* is the Korean word for such bonding. It refers to the attachments that last across generations. These deep attachments always have an ambiguous nature with positive and negative effects. If the relationships formed by *jeong* are betrayed, tremendous hurt can emerge. Sometimes when people want to cut off or get out of relationships, it becomes hard because *jeong* forms over a long time. HyunKyung Chung reports that some Korean women say, "I have too much jeong;" meaning they cannot break oppressive or bad relationships because of *jeong*.

Jeong is foundational for human life because "we are our relationships." Our interactions with those we love and care about create our internal world. Positive *jeong* includes nurturing and caring interpersonal relationships. But *jeong* does not mean the relationship has always been good. When one's relationships have gone through conflict, some Korean people say, "This relationship survived hardships and we are still friends; now you and I have *jeong*." *Jeong* does not require a perfect match with all aspects of others, but a good-enough match with diverse aspects, accepting some ambiguous parts of others and of oneself. This helps to build *jeong*. It is hard to grasp the meaning of *jeong*. Nevertheless, whether positive or negative, *jeong* forges its presence. Koreans have a saying, "It is better to have *mi-eun* [bad] *jeong* than no *jeong*." Absence of *jeong* implies absence of relationship, which means indifference and isolation from others.

Jeong is rooted in relationality, inclusivity, mutuality, and interconnectedness. WonHee Anne Joh argues that *jeong* is a helpful theological idea because it includes not only the positive aspects of love and attachment, but also the abjection of *han*. *Jeong* and *han* belong together as aspects of the experience of human life. Joh finds a significant analogy for the dialectical relationship of *jeong* and *han* in the cross of Christianity. The cross brought together in one moment the deepest human/divine suffering and the deepest human/divine love in the midst of life's contradictions.[3]

Jeong is being appropriated by pastoral theologians as a way to understand the enduring attachments that human beings have for parents, siblings, family members, mentors, teachers, and close friends. Often persons seek pastoral counseling when they experience the full effects of the ambiguities in their important attachments. Following divorce, alienation from parents or children, abuse within the family, and other relationship troubles, persons feel bereft and empty and may suffer depression that threatens personal identity and sometimes survival. The concept of *jeong* can help pastoral caregivers understand the complicated dynamics of relationships.

Salim

Salim is a noun that is related to the verb *salida*, which means to save, rescue, salvage; to safeguard from damage or injury. Some dictionaries translate *salida* into English as "giving things life," "keeping things alive." UnHey Kim says: "Salimsali consists of two different parts, Salim and Sali. The first one is derived from household economy and the latter from house management. Salimsali means all the work and spirit which make things alive."[4]

If one would ask an average Korean about *salim* today, he or she would say, "just women's work in the house." The noun, *salim*, has lost much of its connection with the verb *salida* over time and has come to mean "women's household chores." As such it has become the victim of gender oppression and refers to women's housework such as cooking, cleaning, and repairing clothes, tasks that are culturally devalued because they are assigned to women and servants. *Salim* is often dismissed by those who are privileged because powerful leaders in family and society do not take care of the

---

3. Joh, *Heart of the Cross.* Joh borrowed the term *abjection* from Julia Kristeva.

4. Kim, "Women Leadership in the Korean Salimist Concept," 48.

details. Rather the details are left to those who care for the necessities of life while those who are privileged make "important decisions."

In recent decades, some scholars in feminist, environmental, and theological studies have tried to redeem the word *salim* from its negative associations. They say that the everyday chores of keeping a family healthy and happy are more important than a patriarchal society allows. In fact, taking care of the needs of vulnerable people, such as children, the elderly, the sick, and other people at times when they are hungry and tired, is life giving. These are the everyday chores that Christian theology attempts to hold up as pastoral care or "servant leadership." A recovery of *salim* could show the important link between chores of everyday life and the more lofty positions of public leadership. "I would rather be a doorkeeper in the house of my God than live in the tents of wickedness" (Psalm 84:10). Just as all persons need times of rest and respite, so too the natural environment needs care and protection because of the negative effects of modern economic systems. Certain scholars have worked to retrieve *salim* to refer to care of the earth, animals, plants, and the total ecology. Environmental activism can be seen as an extension of *salim* or pastoral care.[5]

The disciplined practices of *salim* can be quite complex because *salim* requires careful attention to detail and disciplined leadership over years and decades. Professor HeeSung Chung of Ewha University comments on the subtle discernment and nuanced interventions that *salim* must exercise.

> *Salim* is possible only through the ability to cross rigid boundaries and create gaps. The ways of *salim* are flexible. *Salim* could be anything from simple survival to a highly exalted life. Yet, its strategies are various and beyond our imaginations. In a process of *salim*, there are no rigid cleavages and hierarchical orders in terms of setting strategies, practicing religions, and choosing virtues and vices. *Salim* often occurs at trans-boundaries, playing between rules and regulations, and creating enlarged spaces in very narrow places. The process of *salim* is not vertical but spiral, requiring mutual participation of a lot of people.[6]

5. Kim, "Reading the Bible from the Perspective of Korean Women," Kim, *Sangmyungkwa Jachi [Life and Autonomy]*, Lee, *Heankukjuk Sangmyung Shinbak [Korean Life Theology as the Systematic Theology]*. Chung, *Goddess–spell according to HyunKyung*. For a United States reference, see Clinebell, *Ecotherapy*. Graham, *Care of Persons, Care of Worlds*.

6. HeeSung Chung, personal correspondence.

The process of doing *salim* depends on the situation, and a person who engages in *salim*, what HyunKyung Chung calls, a *salimist*,[7] must attend to the everyday reality of people's lives: sitting with a dying person, making clothes for the vulnerable child, building a home for a family in need, preparing a birthday meal for someone who is often overlooked. Many women have been willing to do *salim* because these daily chores are necessary for decent human life, even though their value is denigrated in modern societies. Feminist scholars are working to expand the meaning of *salim* to include care of the congregation, care of the family, care of the environment, and works of peace and justice in the global situation.[8]

Women's work or *salim* has been devalued in Korea because men were expected to engage in productive work while women cared for children and the home. This form of patriarchy existed partly because of the Confucian distinction between *nei* and *wai*, "inside the house" and "outside the house." In traditional Korean culture prior to the twentieth century, outside the house was men's work: meeting the public, engaging in productive work, managing the village, determining issues of public policy, and protecting the family. Inside the house was women's work, *salim*: preparing the meals, cleaning the house, keeping the rituals for the household gods, nurturing the children, and servicing the needs of the head of the house. In its most extreme form, women in elite homes were nearly prisoners in their homes and did not appear in public. When they traveled, they rode in covered carriages with curtains drawn. In working families, the work of women outside in the fields was required for family survival, but the ideal woman was severely restricted to activities inside the home.

In a postmodern society where hierarchies have collapsed, there is no logical reason why inside and outside need to correlate with gender, or why outside should be considered more important than inside. Rather one might understand outside and inside as characteristics of every person and every social system such as a family, a congregation, or a community organization. Each one of us has to differentiate public life and private subjectivity,[9] although these two dimensions should be in close communication so our existence does not become split. Every family has to negotiate with the out-

---

7. Chung, *Goddess-Spell according to HyunKyung.*

8. Kim, "Reading the Bible from the Perspective of Korean Women." Seong Hee Kim, "Rupturing the Empire," 42: Kim, *Sangmyungkwa Jachi [Life and Autonomy]*; Lee, *Hankukjeok Saengmyung Shinhak [Korean Life Theology as Systematic Theology].*

9. Li, *Sage and the Second Sex*, 115–20. In this book, Pauline Lee argues that *nei* and *wai* do not correspond to the Western distinction between public and private.

side world for the resources needed for survival and also encourage nurture and respect for individuals within the family. While gender is often correlated with *yin* and *yang* based in Taoist thought, there is no reason why *yin* should be female and *yang* male within a postmodern society. For both genders, *yin* and *yang* can be understood as the dynamic interchange of the full range of human characteristics such as sadness and happiness, hope and despair, empathy and aggression, etc. Inside and outside can have a yin and yang relationship: like any polarity, the two poles are always found together and whenever one is dominant, it is already yielding to the other, and whenever one is subordinate, it is already asserting itself to restore the balance. "An Eastern Asian philosophy such as Daoism, originally does not contain any concept of dualistic domination. It emphasizes the balance and unity of nature, which includes the human being as a part of it."[10]

Nei and *wai* have a dialectical relationship with one another, and involve a dynamic interplay for every person, family, and social system. A healthy person will attend to self-care of body, mind, and spirit and also engage in creative work with others in the larger community. Healthy families and communities care for the security, health and nurture of its vulnerable members and also engage in collaborative work with other families on joint projects and missions in the world. These two sides of human experience, inside and outside, do not correlate with gender: men are called to be both creative workers and caregivers for others; and women are called to active leadership in the larger community and to actions of care for those who are vulnerable. Therefore, inside and outside are necessary for balance and flexibility in human life. While *salim* has traditionally been considered the work of inside (women's household chores), *salim and salida,* giving life, are characteristic of both inside and outside.

Salim can be a helpful concept for pastoral theologians as a way to understand the processes of healing for persons and families. In some ways, *salim* refers to the everyday work that human beings should value as they respond to the *han* and *jeong* in their lives. As intercultural dialogue continues, *salim* may be a helpful analogy for healing, nurturing, sustaining, and reconciling our communities in the midst of the threats of death,

10. Kim, "Reading the Bible from the Perspective of Korean Women," 49. Rosenlee, *Confucianism and Women.* See especially chapter four, 'Nei–Wai, Gender Distinctions, and Ritual Propriety." Ko, Haboush, and Piggott, eds., *Women and Confucian Cultures in Premodern China, Korea, and Japan.*

alienation, and oppression. *Salim* could become a synonym for pastoral care of persons and worlds.[11]

Summary

The concepts of *han, jeong,* and *salim* offer clues to Korean spirituality. *Han* gives the people a way to understand what Park and Nelson call "the sinned against,"[12] and what Mercandante calls "anguish."[13] We don't have an English word for the deep suffering of people who are oppressed over generations. We use words such as suffering, trauma, and oppression, but they don't carry the same combination of nuances as *han.* Likewise, *jeong* refers to the deeper connections that survive the ambiguities and alienation that are part of many relationships and systems. *Salim* could become a way to describe the practices of healing and care that are part of all human creativity.

Han, Jeong, and *Salim* in Relation to the Christian Trinity

Whenever one engages in intercultural and interreligious conversation, there is a correlation of ideas between two distinct forms of belief and practice. Some ideas share an identity, some are dissimilar or contradictory, and some are analogous, that is, they present complementary perspectives about common human realities.[14] Having identified *han, jeong, and salim* as ideas that some Korean scholars have brought into pastoral theology, we attempt to correlate these ideas with the Western theology of God as Trinity. We offer these thoughts as an invitation to further conversations across lines of culture, religions, and theological perspectives.

11. Graham, *Care of Persons, Care of Worlds.*

12. Park and Nelson, *Other Side of Sin.*

13. Mercandante, *Victims and Sinners.*

14. Tracy, "Practical Theology in the Situation of Global Pluralism," in *Formation and Reflection,* 139.

God as Creator, Parent

God as creator suggests that we find ourselves already in a web of relationships that we did not create and the subject of relational forces that we cannot ignore. We did not make ourselves, but were created by an Other; and we were formed through others who came before us. Without these others, we would not exist. Finding ourselves in the midst of relationships that determine our very existence is the starting point for human faith and piety. We become human through our attachments to significant people, institutions, and ideas. The Korean concept of *jeong* expresses this reality well. We develop our identity as persons during childhood in response to the people who take care of us. We transform our identities during adolescence and adulthood through nurturing relationships with family, teachers, mentors, and peers. Our lives are embedded in our relationships

The Korean concept of *jeong* is always characterized by ambiguity. We experience conflicts and contradictions in our important relationships that present challenges for identity. As Christians who follow Jesus we are called to increase the positive *jeong* in our relationships and diminish the negative *jeong*. *Jeong* expresses what many pastoral theologians have discovered in intensive work with others: that we live in the midst of ambiguous relationships that require understanding and healing.

However, within modernity, whether in Korea or the United States, individuals often try to erase any sense of relationship or dependence on others. In the minds of many, individuals just *are*, and they feel they owe their existence to nothing or no one. Relationships are necessary because individuals bump up against others who also exist. In the process of bumping against one another, some relationships become useful as we strive to assert our existence and some relationships are threatening. Since we exist by accident, we can just as easily not exist. So individuals are always striving to enhance their existence in cooperation and competition with the striving of others. Within this modern way of thinking, relationships are utilitarian, that is, they have no necessary meaning unless they help or hinder the individual in reaching some internal goal. The life and death of others is unimportant except as it affects the happiness of the individual.

This utilitarian view of relationships often shows up in theology. One version of this philosophy even views our relationship with God as solely utilitarian. We love God because God blesses us; and God blesses us because we believe in God. Faith is a matter of reward and punishment. If we worship and obey God we will be rewarded; if we do not worship and obey

God, we will be punished. If we are faithful we go to heaven; if not we go to hell. This popular theology in the United States and Korea is thoroughly modern. It is based on the assumption that our relationships are secondary to our being, and all relationships are utilitarian, that is, they are good if they serve our self-interest. Our faith in God can be understood as an extension of our striving to enhance our precarious existence. For Christians living in modern cultures, ideas of relationship are problematic. On the one hand, we live out of the classical creeds that emphasize our dependence upon God and our need for acceptance of God's sovereignty in our lives. On the other hand, we live in a modern culture that promotes individualism, autonomy, and self-interest.

In contrast, believing in God as the creator of our relationships means accepting our earthly lives as gifts of God and working to increase love among all people. In this context, the Korean concept of *jeong* has a contribution to make. *Jeong* is about acknowledging and honoring the relationships that have given us our being. Asian beliefs encourage the honoring of parents and those before them because all people come from their parents' bodies and spirits. We have *jeong* or attachment with our ancestors, for better or worse. Behind those who gave us physical and often emotional life is God the ultimate ancestor, who called us into being and gives us the structure of our lives. To honor God and our ancestors is to honor our very being because we are our relationships. When we have faith and engage in fervent prayer, we nurture a relationship of *jeong* with God. If we do not honor God and our ancestors, then we do not honor ourselves and we will not have respect for our offspring: our children, our students, and others who look to us for guidance. Honoring our relationships and engaging in rituals to express that honor is central to a life filled with *jeong*. How we honor our ancestors in the midst of the contradictions and ambiguities they passed on to us is one of the deepest challenges of human life.

For Koreans, rituals to honor parents and ancestors are part of everyday life. Children bow to their parents throughout their life; students bow to their teachers when they see them; and in Korean churches, bowing to one another replaces the traditional greeting of a handshake and/ or a kiss during the time of sharing. Bowing shows honor, respect, and gratitude for the influence of the others. At specific times, more elaborate rituals of respect are enacted by some families, including visits to ancestor graves. These rituals remind families of their embeddedness in a long history of persons who have given them life. And behind these ancestors is the Ultimate Other who gives all life—God, who Korean Christians call *Hananim*. Before the twentieth century, many Korean families had shrines in their homes to remind them of the spirits who were around them every day, and daily respect was shown to these spirits because they gave persons their lives. The first missionaries forbade Korean Christians from practicing these rituals, and most families do not practice ancestor veneration today. However, while ancestor veneration was a form of political ideology that may have fostered oppression of many people in the late nineteenth century, the missionaries probably misjudged its deeper meaning.

To have respect for ourselves, we need to honor others, especially parents and other family members who gave us our start in life. However, our relationships always come to us as an ambiguous mixture of *han* and *jeong*. Our bodies and spirits feel the accumulated *han* over generations, and we struggle to find healing for the suffering we have inherited and experienced in our bodies and relationships. *Jeong* is the attachment to life we feel because others have loved us and sacrificed so we might thrive. Korean parents are known to make sacrifices so that their children will have access to education and blessings even though they will never be able to fully participate with them or enjoy the benefits. Those who have immigrated to the United States often give up professional careers and spend the rest of their lives laboring in dry cleaning or restaurant work so their children can be lawyers and doctors. Parents sacrifice out of their feelings of *jeong* for their children. But out of this sacrifice also come new layers of *han* as children become alienated from their parents and their cultures.

God has thrown us into a precarious life of relationships with other persons and with our creator. We give honor to God when we value the relational web that is God's creation. As Saint Paul preached to the Athenians: "From one ancestor [God] made all nations to inhabit the whole earth, and [God] allotted the times of their existence and the boundaries of the places where they would live, so that they would search for God and perhaps grope for [God] and find [God]—though indeed [God] is not far from each one of us. For 'In [God] we live and move and have our being;' as even some of your own poets have said, 'For we too are [God's] offspring.'" (Acts 17:26–28)

Jesus Christ as Redeemer and Savior

A second basic belief of Christians is that we live within a cycle of life, death, and resurrection. Jesus Christ, the second person of the Trinity, lived as a human on earth, suffered persecution and death, and rose from the grave to eternal life. Because we believe in Jesus and accept his revelation of the nature of God, we live in faith that God transforms our existence through cycles of life, death, and resurrection. These phases of life express our relationship with our physical bodies and our everyday thoughts and actions. We receive our life from our relationships and we become emotionally attached to certain people and projects. We give ourselves to people and projects as forms of self-creation and creativity for others. We hope that the process of receiving life from others and giving life to others will contribute to greater harmony, peace, and prosperity for all.

However, we know also that the relationships we receive are filled with *han*. The challenge of being human is to receive the full impact of our relationships and respond with love so that all life moves toward greater harmony and beauty. However, this dynamic of receptivity and creativity inevitably involves suffering because the full complexity of our relationships includes much grief and violence—grief over what has been lost and violence as systems of domination assert themselves at the expense of persons who are vulnerable. There is inevitable suffering for those who are attached to the full reality of the world as it is, and additional suffering is required when we work to harmonize these contradictions for the future. Christian faith teaches us that if we love life and our relationships and work to harmonize the contradictions for the sake of healing and beauty, the miracle of resurrection is possible. Even though we often cannot see the results of love while we are in the midst of the challenges of life, new life is being born and will be more beautiful than we can imagine. The cycle of life, death, and resurrection is basic to faith in Jesus Christ.

Modernity disrupts this guiding truth about the nature of reality. Isolated individuals without real relationships are incapable of genuine love, and the work of love to harmonize the relational contradictions for the sake of peace and justice makes no sense. Instead, modernity teaches that self-interest is the guiding principle of human life, and that the competitive striving for acquisition of goods and power will fuel the market economy for the benefit of all. There is no need for a guiding myth about love, suffering, and resurrection because the free markets will take care of everything. Modernity accepts the greed and selfishness of individuals as the reality upon which to base its mythology. When rebellion arises because of the injustice of capitalistic markets, the state uses violence to protect its interests, often at the expense of persons and communities without political power. Premodern states that insist on old-fashioned morality and control are interpreted as obstacles to progress and often intimidated so that the markets can thrive. This abusive use of state power is justified by the phrase, "collateral damage," for the larger purpose of sustaining global market capitalism.

The Korean terms discussed above—*jeong, han,* and *salim*—have analogies to Christian beliefs about life, death, and resurrection. While they are not exact parallels, the conversation can enrich our understanding of both ways of thinking. *Jeong* is analogous to a key concept in relational theology: "attachment to life."[15] Through our parents and ancestors God has given us life. As Heidegger said, we are thrown into our life situation. When we become conscious of being selves, we find ourselves embedded in a web of relationships that make us who we are. Whether our relationships are positive or negative, most human beings hope to contribute to healing and wholeness in the future by treating others and ourselves with respect. As Jesus and several Asian sages taught, you should "love your neighbor as yourself."[16]

However, the relationships we inherit are full of trouble. To love others with whom we have *jeong* is a complicated challenge. Those who influenced us passed on many troubles because they could not resolve the issues in their own lives and communities. We will not be able to resolve many of our own contradictions and will pass them on to others. *Jeong,* for many Korean people, includes this mixture of love and suffering. We have no choice about the *jeong* we were born into, and we are called to live the life we have been given; so we must choose how to respond with love and care to what we have received. *Jeong* is attachment that includes the ambiguity of life

15. "Jesus had what theologian Bernard Meland calls 'an attachment to life.' Within process theology, this means that Jesus was able to give his full attention to the flow of the human experiences of others in all their complexity, and to respond creatively in ways that revealed a quality of truth and value that set people free" (Poling, *Rethinking Faith,* 58).

16. Matthew 7:12: "In everything do to others as you would have them do to you; for this is the law and the prophets." Tzu-Kung asked, "Is there a single word which can be a guide to conduct throughout one's life?" The Master replied: "It is perhaps the word 'shu' [reciprocity]: Do not impose on others what you yourself do not desire" (Confucius, *Analects* XV 24 135). "Regard your neighbor's gain as your own gain, and your neighbor's loss as your own loss" (Lao Tzu, *T'ai Shang Kan Ying P'ien,* 213–18), online: http://www.bessel.org/golden.htm.

and relationships. When Jesus came into the world, he found himself in the midst of violence, oppression, and suffering. King Herod killed all the baby boys of Bethlehem because he feared that the birth of a king would threaten his rule and privileges. Many of the people in Jesus's own community were poor, sick, mentally ill, and oppressed. He accepted fully the reality of the world into which he was born, and engaged in ministries of healing those with physical illness, casting out evil demons, and preaching about God's love for all people. In the same way, we are each born into a world with its own set of problems and troubles. We should respond with *jeong*, that is, with loving attachment to the people and the world in which we live, doing our best to love and heal for the sake of justice. Christians believe that God acts with *jeong* in relation to humans and the world.

Han is the deep sadness that comes when we feel the full impact of the ambiguities that make up our life. Unless we allow ourselves to feel *han*, we cannot understand the full extent of the suffering inherited from the past and the ongoing suffering of ourselves and the people around us. *Han* is painful, and human beings tend to avoid pain if possible. When we touch a hot stove, the pain in our hand tells us to remove it quickly from danger. Pain is a signal that something is wrong and needs to be corrected. Unfortunately, one way to respond to pain is to ignore or deny the reality of what we feel. Rather than receive the suffering of the world, we can deny the reality of that pain, close our eyes, and refuse to understand it. In contrast, God invites us to enter fully into the existential and historic pain that comes to us through our relationships.

The *han* of Jesus's community was related to the poverty and oppression of the people under Roman colonization and the betrayal and collaboration by their own religious and political leaders. Through his teachings, parables, and miracles, he disclosed this suffering for all to see and offered a new vision of abundant life in a new kingdom. When Jesus showed that the suffering of the people was a result of oppression and called for a new kingdom, he was feared and hated by the religious and political leaders and eventually murdered by the government for blasphemy and sedition. The crucifixion of Jesus reveals the full reality of *han* in the world, what Joh calls abjection. The cross is a symbol of the mixture of love and abjection, *jeong* and *han*. Even though he was innocent of any crime, the state put him to a painful death in order to stop his social movement and secure its own power. By accepting the *han* of the world of his time with love, Jesus chose to express his attachment to life even when it led to his own suffering and death. Jesus was not personally responsible for the *han* of the world, but he chose to take the cross imposed on him as a form of identification with all people.

As Christians, we are called to embrace the *han* of our time. Because we live in a different time than Jesus, the *han* we feel will be different from the *han* Jesus felt. We have to accept the personal and global suffering of our time and seek responses that are appropriate to these contradictions in hope that our embrace of suffering will contribute to healing and harmony for the future. God knows *han* because God identifies with the suffering of humans and the world.

Salim-salida is the possibility of new life in the midst of love and suffering. *Salim* is the ongoing practice of life giving and peacemaking in response to the *jeong* and *han* of the world we live in. When Jesus healed and taught the people, he showed care by focusing on the everyday sufferings of people who had no status in society. He died a criminal's death because he defended the powerless against those who had worldly power. Jesus's death reveals God's identification with the deep suffering and pain of this world. In this sense, Jesus died for us. In the same way, Jesus' resurrection is for all people. Jesus' life, death, and resurrection overturn the concepts of power and control exercised in the world and bring a new community of inclusive love and justice for all. Thus, we can see in the word *salim* the possibility of new life coming out of death in the same way that the resurrection of Jesus came out of the crucified death he suffered.

Part of the beauty of *salim* is that it involves working for new life and resurrection in the midst of everyday reality. Christians sometimes call this "living the resurrection faith." Zen Buddhists have a saying, "Wash the cup and put it away," meaning that life goes on through the mundane details of everyday life, including the reality of suffering and death.[17] Traditional Confucian rituals of death emphasize the importance of children being with their parents when they die, then washing and wrapping the body with respect and dignity and moving to burial within twenty-four to seventy-two hours, as soon as the family can gather. When ancient communities heard of death, the whole village used to gather and sit with the family day and night for three days. Recently, in Korea a seminary faculty member's

---

17. "A monk told Joshu: 'I have just entered the monastery. Please teach me.' Joshu asked: 'Have you eaten your rice porridge?' The monk replied: 'I have eaten.' Joshu said: 'Then you had better wash your bowl.' At that moment the monk was enlightened." (Zen Koan # 7 from Yamada, *The Gateless Gate*; online: http://www.sacred-texts.com/bud/glg/glg07.htm/).

father died. As soon as colleagues heard about the death, they got into cars and drove four hours to be with the family. They arrived at 1:00 a.m., stayed for several hours, and then drove back to the seminary to continue their teaching. The solidarity of the family and community in times of death symbolizes *salim* and resurrection.

On the anniversary of a death, the family gathers and pays honor to the deceased, pledging to continue to remember and keep the family vision alive in the way they live and behave. Eternal life is symbolized in the ancestor rituals that teach children to honor the family and keep the values and dreams of the family alive for future generations. God does *salim* within the creation, giving life in the mundane everyday details that make up our being. And in our grief over the death of a parent, relative, or friend, life goes on. In our little deaths of relationships, projects, disappointments, betrayals, human life is resilient. God's love is resilient. God makes *salim* possible. Through *salim*, the resilient spirits of God and humans survive and live for another day when healing, harmony, and beauty are again possible.

Pastoral counseling deals with the life, death and resurrection cycles of the everyday lives of people who come for care because their hopes for abundant life are threatened. Persons seek out pastors because they have hope for the life they believe is possible in Jesus Christ, even though they experience suffering and disappointment. The goal of counseling is reaffirming their hope, identifying with their suffering, and affirming the little resurrections that might be overlooked. In effective pastoral counseling that responds to the depth of people's pain, the result will be an increase in hope and faith in spite of suffering and in the midst of everyday life.

The Holy Spirit: Empowerment for Healing and Reconciliation

The third person of the Trinity is the Holy Spirit, healing and empowering us as we strive to be faithful. God creates our lives through relationships; Jesus redeems us through the cycle of living, dying, and rising again; the Spirit sustains us, healing us in the midst of our relationships and empowering us for our ministries of love. The power of the spirit allows us to be attached to our relationships, to survive the cycles of hurt and violence that come to us, and to trust in the resilience of life after death.

"The Holy Spirit . . . is the power that raises the dead, the power of the new creation of all things; and faith is the beginning of the rebirth of human beings to new life. But this means that the Holy Spirit is by no means merely a matter of revelation. It has to do with life and its source. The Holy Spirit is called 'holy' . . . because it sanctifies life and renews the face of the earth."[18] Through *jeong, han,* and *salim* Korean spirituality contributes to our understanding of the spirits and the work of the Holy Spirit.

A common saying among Koreans is "We are emotional people." Sometimes the emotionality of Koreans is not apparent in the United States because native English speakers often meet immigrants who are self-conscious about learning English or second generation Korean Americans who have adopted United States culture as their own. But in Korea, the emotional nature of the people is apparent in language, gestures, music, worship, and religion. The same Koreans who defer to age and status with bows and respect have overthrown kings and presidents and suffered martyrdom because of resistance to tyrants of various kinds. The range of emotions permitted in Korean culture is not the same as the repressed emotionality of many northern European immigrants who were the ancestors of Protestants in the United States.

Koreans love classical European music and Italian opera, but the favorites in concerts and on the radio are often emotional and romantic pieces that bring tears to one's eyes. The traditional court music of the elite is slow and dignified, but *Sa-Mul-No-Ri*, "farmer's music," is boisterous, with drums, gongs, and traditional instruments.[19]

In keeping with the tradition, most Koreans believe in the world of spirits. Churches show strong Pentecostal influence in their prayers, music, and responses to preaching. Pentecostal faith is based on the reality of spirits. The Holy Spirit brings healing, ecstasy, and empowerment for believers; evil spirits bring testing, suffering, and disaster on vulnerable people, including the faithful at times.

Many Koreans call on the services of shamanistic *mudangs* at times of important family or business decisions, or when there is illness or an economic problem. Christians are particularly unlikely to talk about this part of their lives because it is not approved by the churches. But the popular media and scholarly literature are full of stories about shamanistic rituals. When there is a problem in a family or business, shamans believe that the spirits are unhappy with the family in some way. Sometimes ritual inadequacy

18. Moltmann, *The Spirit of Life.* 7–8.

19. "Korean traditional music can be roughly divided into two major categories, chong-ak and sog-ak: music for the ruling class and for the common people, respectively" ("Korean Music").

has made an ancestor unhappy, and the misfortune has been sent to get the family's attention and bring them back into communication with the spirit world. At other times the ancestors have sent the misfortune because of a family conflict that has not been addressed, or one that endangers the family. For simple questions, the *mudang* or other shaman can perform rituals of a few hours or give advice about where to build a house or open a business. For more complicated problems, such as the chronic illness of a child, a divorce, family violence, or bankruptcy, a *gut* of a day or several days is required. Some scholars have analyzed these prolonged rituals and suggested that they function as a kind of family therapy. The *mudang* enters into a trance and becomes a mediator between the family and the spirit world. In trance, she can speak on behalf of the family to the spirits, or she can speak to the family on behalf of the spirits. Sometimes these conversations are quite emotional and even abusive as the spirits communicate their deepest feelings. The effect of the longer rituals can be a transformation of the family structure and dynamics. An abusive member can be confronted and told to respect the family more; a depressed person can be comforted and challenged to be more active in the family; an alienated relationship between husband and wife, brother and brother, mother-in-law and daughter-in-law can be examined and changed. An effective *mudang* will have a intuitive sense of the family dynamics and provide help.[20]

From five thousand years of history, what have Koreans learned about the spirits that can help others understand the work of the Holy Spirit in our time?

First, humans must give honor to the spirits, first through ancestors, and eventually to the gods and the Most High God, *Hananim*. The modern idea that there are no spirits in the world is a dangerous one. Koreans believe that it matters to the spirits whether living human beings give them the honor that is their due. Korean traditional religions have many rituals that serve this purpose.

Second, as we honor the spirits, we should also give honor to one another. "Love one another with mutual affection; outdo one another in showing honor."[21] Korean society has sometimes fostered the idea that honor is a one-way relationship from subject to king, child to parent, wife to

---

20. For the perspective of scholars on Korean Shamanism, see part 3, on Shamanism, in Buswell, ed., *Religions of Korea in Practice*, 233–354 (chapters 14–19). See also Hogarth, *Korean Shamanism and Cultural Nationalism*.

21. Romans 12:10.

husband. But in a postmodern society where hierarchies are relativized, the basic function of a political leader is to honor her or his subjects and decide policies with benevolence for their benefit. Subjects should give honor to political leaders who are trustworthy in their work on behalf of the people. Parents should respect their children as gifts of God so that their children will gain respect for themselves and others. Married partners should honor one another and work together to foster the creativity of each other. When we honor one another in love, then we promote a cooperative society. The purpose of rituals is to harmonize the often turbulent interaction of humans for the common good.

Third, we need to honor our attachments of *jeong,* the deep love and ambivalence we have for family and friends, and extend our *jeong* to all people. In Christian literature in the United States there is a debate about the nature of love. Many Christians insist that agape love means unselfish, sacrificial love for all people regardless of our relationship to them or their status in society. In Western ethics, following the thought of Immanuel Kant, impartiality is often considered the greatest moral virtue. Confucius thought this a foolish idea. It is a matter of common sense that we give our greatest care to those we care about the most about. We give honor to our parents and their parents because they gave us life. We give honor to our children and their children because they represent our legacy for the future. We give honor to those we live with every day and try to empower them to do their best. Beyond our important attachments, we also give honor by granting people their human status in the world. We learn to honor all people by first giving honor to those close to us. If we neglect to honor our own parents, how would we know the appropriate honor to give to a stranger?

> Although *ren* [love] begins in the family and in family relationships its final destination is the general others . . . Mencius explains the move in this way: "Treat the aged (*lao*) in a manner befitting their venerable age and extend this treatment to the aged of others families; treat your own young (*yui*) in a manner befitting their tender age and extend this to the young of other families . . . In other words, all you have to do is take this very mind here and apply it to what is over there. Hence, one who extends his bounty (*tui'en*) can bring peace to the four seas, one who does not cannot bring peace even to his own family.[22]

22. Tao, "Two Perspectives of Care," 224.

In fact, it is through honoring our parents and love relationships that we come to know the meaning of honor and love itself. By honoring those close to us we grow in our understanding of honor so we can also give appropriate honor to those far off. Confucius was angry at religious monks who neglected to honor their parents because of their religious commitments. What kind of love is this, that religious people neglect aging parents in poverty in order to give charity for strangers? The spirits are the ones who give us *jeong*, attachment to others, and encourage us to live in these relationships with honor.[23]

Fourth, the spirits are concerned about justice. When misfortune falls on a family, it is usually because of an injustice in the family, or between the family and the ancestors. Within the shamanistic world, misfortune is a sign that relationships are unjust. The task of a good shaman is to discern the injustice and create a family drama that brings healing to the system because of the injustice. The sensitive shamans develop rituals that help people reenact the proper relationships of respect and love that they need in order to handle the challenges of life. Of course, there are unethical shamans, just as there are unethical pastors and kings, who prescribe meaningless rituals so they can collect fees for their own support. But there is an ethical system within Shamanism that is about honor and healing for the sake of justice. A human being treated with disrespect and violence tears apart the whole system and causes suffering.

The movie *Fast Runner* tells a story about an indigenous Alaskan community and how it deals with a murder within the community. For many months, the community is not clear on what happened and is unsure what to do. But eventually the truth comes out. In a kind of *gut*, the community engages in truth telling about the incident and decides on the solution. The oldest elder gives the community consensus and pronounces the consequence: the banishment of the murderers from the community. For the men who committed the murder, separation from the community is a terrible outcome because their identities were so connected to the community. But only banishment could restore the injustice caused by the violent death of one of the precious members of the community. The whole community grieved the death of the member and the banishment of two other

---

23. For additional commentary on the idea that human beings should first honor their parents and family before they honor strangers, see Baker, "Introduction," in Buswell, ed., *Religions of Korea in Practice*, 21–23; and Tu, *Confucian Thought*, 95.

members. This outcome is much different from the legalistic and disinterested criminal justice systems in most modern nations.[24]

In the work of spirits in Korean culture, we see *jeong, han,* and *salim* at work. Human beings are spirits, minds, and bodies, and we live in a world filled with the spirits of others who are living on earth, passed on, and yet to come.[25] We have *jeong* with these spirits that we need to honor, so we can learn how to honor our own spirit and the spirits of other people. God comes to us as spirit, encouraging us to love and care for one another. This spiritual world is characterized by collective *han,* which has accumulated through history. The trauma and suffering of the past are not over, but they are carried with us in our bodies and spirits. When we honor the spirits, we will feel both the attachment and the suffering that we have inherited. How we respond to the love and suffering is central to our call to be faithful to the life God has given us. Our ministry as human beings is to practice *salim,* peacemaking, care giving, and life giving. *Salim* is the work of the Holy Spirit which we are called to join. When we are empowered by the Holy Spirit, we will be able to feel the *jeong* and *han* of our lives and practice *salim* for ourselves, others, and God.

When people turn to pastoral counselors, they are responding to God's call. They sense, perhaps intuitively, the discrepancy between their lives and the claim of God on them. Their hope is frustrated by oppression from others and by their own self-defeating feelings and behaviors. They seek spiritual companionship so they can understand the ministry to which God is calling them. Many theories of pastoral counseling speak of the presence of the Holy Spirit as a third person in the conversation, seeking ways of understanding and responding to the complicated relationships and overwhelming suffering. When pastoral counseling is effective, the pastor will often feel the presence of the Spirit. One of the rewards of pastoral counseling is seeing the Holy Spirit at work in the lives of persons who were formerly depressed, anxious, and fearful.

24. The movie *Fast Runner* (*Atanarjuat*) was produced within an indigenous community in Arctic Canada and released in 2001.

25. There are some interesting analogies between Korean spirit-world and indigenous African cosmologies. Berinyuu, *Towards Theory and Practice of Pastoral Counseling in Africa.*

Summary and Conclusion

Jeong, han, and *salim* have potential for enriching and deepening basic theological concepts of pastoral theology. The pastoral care and counseling ministries of the church depend on our understandings of God's love and power in relation to humans and the creation. *Jeong* can help Western caregivers understand the depth and ambiguities of human relationships that make up our everyday lives and shape our identities. Attachments within relationships are always complex, and *jeong* helps us see this complexity as resource and challenge. *Han* can help Western caregivers understand the depth and complexity of suffering, and the importance and difficulty of responding to the trauma in human individuals, families, and communities. Because *han* accumulates over generations and is passed down from parents to children, its roots in the trauma of the past are often obscure. Caregivers need to help persons discover the family and cultural history of violence, trauma, depression, addiction, and other stresses that affect their lives, and help them to avoid being controlled by the sadness, rage, and fear of this history. Suffering needs healing that can only come through honest appraisal of narratives and relationships. *Salim* can help Western caregivers see that the drive for abundant life, harmony, and peace comes through everyday events. How we organize our daily lives, who we spend our time with, how we attend to the everyday beauty around us—these are questions of *salim*. We find peace and harmony when we pay attention to the realities embedded in relationships.

In this chapter we have discussed key concepts of Korean spirituality and their relationship to Western Christian theology. We focused our attention on the values of *han, jeong,* and *salim*. We then discussed analogies between these ideas and the Christian Trinitarian God and found points of connection that could be resources for a postmodern pastoral care and counseling. It is apparent that *han, jeong,* and *salim* bring important insights that can enrich and enlarge Western understandings of pastoral theology.

In the next chapter, HeeSun Kim engages in intercultural conversation, integrating her experience of growing up in Korea with what she has learned from Western theology by studying in Korea and the United States. Her work provides a second illustration of the rich dialogue that is possible when one takes seriously Korean contributions to pastoral theology.

7

A Constructive Intercultural Pastoral Theology

AFTER EXPLORING KOREAN HISTORY and spirituality, we try to find places where the Korean concepts of *han, jeong,* and *salim* can contribute to pastoral theology. Our specific concern in this chapter is to enrich the meaning of the Trinity with *han, jeong,* and *salim,* especially for the sake of Christian women.

As a Korean feminist pastoral theologian studying Western theology, I, HeeSun Kim, try to find and retrieve helpful ideas from Korean culture in order to construct a conversation between Korean concepts and Western Christian faith. Similar efforts have been made in chapter six by James Poling as a Western white male pastoral theologian. The reader can evaluate how our attempts are different and similar and valuable to each other from our own contexts.

Some traditional Christian dogma has been toxic to women who are in the midst of abusive situations; I want to believe, then, some other values should detoxify. Since many abused Christian women's thorny questions are about the meaning of suffering and the cross, I explore how the Korean concepts of *han, jeong, and salim,* in dialogue with the Trinity, can make contributions to the field of pastoral care and ultimately to many Christian women.

Salim Trinity: Human Suffering and the Trinitarian God

"Be obedient just like Jesus when he endured suffering and death on the cross. If you go through the suffering, you will have a reward at the end. You must die first in order to live." These words can be painful for any person to hear. I have heard those teachings through sermons and teachings in church, and many Christians continue to hear these words. Endurance of suffering is a deeply embedded virtue for Christians, especially for women. I remember one episode that happened not long ago.

> One night, I got a phone call. The woman seemed insecure. She said she got my number from her friend since she wanted to talk to a pastor. She revealed a lot of information and sought religious perspectives for her suffering. The woman told me that her husband had beaten her from the beginning of their marriage and she is in her fifties now. She told me that she felt obligated to stay with him since she was a Christian and wanted to be a good Christian. I asked her what being a Christian meant to her. She answered that a Christian meant bearing one's cross as Jesus did. A good Christian woman would be willing to accept personal pain because Jesus didn't turn away from suffering. Therefore, she did not seem to want to take any particular action to fix her situation. Rather, she seemed to want to hear confirming words from me that would sustain this faith during this abusive relationship, such as, "Yes, you need to bear your cross." I think I could have helped her more if the Christian tradition taught something other than the virtue of suffering and forgiveness. When she hung up she said she would call me again.

My interest in regard to exploring questions about God arises when I ask, "What image of God faithfully communicates with the lives of Christians today, particularly shattered women?" In order to answer this question, I critically look at what has influenced the understanding of suffering for Christian women. I ask how feminist theologians should respond to this understanding of suffering in relation to its effects on Christian women and whether there is a possibility of new understandings of God. In this process, I have met three feminist and womanist theologians who claim that the Triune God can help to answer these thorny theodicy questions.

The Questions in the Midst of Suffering: Why Me? Where and Who Is God?

A person who is victimized by abuse frequently asks the questions, why me? and, where is God? These two simple sentences cannot be answered simply. The suffering in a world created by a loving God is quite disturbing.

In the presence of extreme violence, it is inevitable that one's faith is tested. Who is God in a world of suffering?

These questions of theodicy continue. If God provides for the well-being of all creation, then why is there evil in the world and why is there so much violence toward others? It is difficult to respond to the "why" questions. Some people ask about the cause of suffering and some ask about the meaning or purpose of suffering. In any case, people ask God for an explanation for the suffering.

In response to such philosophical questions, James Cone provides a different perspective. He argues, " The main reason theologians have said little that can be used in the struggle of the oppressed is due to the fact that they have been only spectators and not victims of suffering."[1] Instead of the metaphysical speculation, Cone tries to understand God in the concrete contexts of black people through their suffering and oppression; he declares that God sides with the oppressed. Cone's claim is resonant with many marginalized groups' concerns, including women.

However, his notion of suffering has side effects that might lead to valorizing suffering. Cone sees suffering as an inevitable consequence of faith, stating, "Faith is born out of suffering."[2] But I argue it can be quite harmful to some Christian women who suffer from their abusive husbands; it may lead many women to actual death.

Many classic theologies reinforce women's oppression and encourage them to see their suffering as redemptive. For many, the cross is a symbol of suffering. Identifying with the sufferings of Jesus on the cross has contributed to women remaining as victims. It encourages many women in abusive situations to identify themselves with the atoning and crucified Christ.

Feminists are critical of the linking of the destructive suffering with the will of God. Mary Daly was the first feminist theologian who pointed out the negative effect of valorizing the suffering of women. "The qualities that Christianity idealizes, especially for women, are also those of the victims; sacrificial love, passive acceptance of suffering, humility, meekness, etc. Since these are the qualities idealized in Jesus 'who died for our sins,' his functioning as a model reinforces the scapegoat syndrome for women."[3] Suffering is thereby sanctioned in Christian life. The woman who wants to be a sincere Christian may decide to endure suffering like Jesus who suf-

1. Cone, *God of the Oppressed*, 166.

2. Ibid., xvii–xviii.

3. Daly, *Beyond God the Father*, 77.

fered for us all. But this glorification of suffering encourages women who are being abused to care more about their abusers than themselves.

When suffering comes many women ask, 'Where is God leading me?' since they have learned at church that every event is part of God's bigger plan that eventually will end with triumph. The reality is that victimization does not always lead to triumph. Some victimization brings more pain if it is not refused or fought against; it can lead to destruction of the human spirit by losing a person's sense of power, worth and dignity. And violence can lead to actual death.

Some Christian women may hope that their cruel husbands may eventually be converted by this sweet acceptance of abuse in the manner of Jesus. This double bind of deserved suffering for guilt and the promise of becoming a Christ-like agent of redemption for one's victimizers through innocent suffering has been a powerful message that Christian women have found very difficult to challenge.[4]

Some theologies leave the impression that God is omnipotent, impassible, immutable and all loving. Since this God is not quite connected with the actual contexts of suffering, women feel abandoned by God. Another alternative is that women abandon God. Do we have any other choice except feeling abandoned by God or abandoning God? Another choice is found in the Trinity, some theologians say.

Some Preliminary Works: Bridge to the Trinity

God is more than two men and a bird. (SANDRA SCHNEIDERS)[5]

"I believe in God, the Father, the Son, and Holy Spirit.' In the traditional doctrine of the Trinity God is one, but there is diversity. The idea of one and diversity in God is still confusing and mysterious to many Christians.

Not all theologians take the doctrine of the Trinity seriously. Yet there are many attempts to make the connection between the Trinity and human suffering, such as the claim that the Trinity responds to human suffering differently than the one God who is imagined as a monarch. Many feminist theologians try to embrace and retrieve the meaning of the Trinity. They say the doctrine of the Trinity can help to overcome monarchism and androcentrism in God. The dynamic of the three persons is a challenge to

4. Ruether, *Introducing Redemption*, 100.

5. Schneiders, "God Is More than Two Men and a Bird."

philosophies of the One God as monarch; it challenges and reshapes the male-centered character of the Father and the Son. In addition, it provides richer implications for our lives in relationship since Trinitarian theology is more sensitive to human suffering and requires human cooperation in God's work.[6]

For more elaboration, I briefly introduce three feminist and woman-ist theologians and their work on the Trinity: Catherine LaCugna, Karen Baker-Fletcher, and Elizabeth Johnson.

Three Feminist Theologians' Understanding of the Trinity

The three feminist theologians reviewed here all see the Trinity through the concept of *perichoresis,* a term used by the Greek theologian John Damascene in the eighth century to emphasize the dynamic character of each person in the Trinity. Catherine LaCugna and Elizabeth Johnson re-interpret this concept for a contemporary audience, especially for women. *Perichoresis* means "being-in-another, permeation without confusion."[7] The word in its original Greek has a particular advantage as an image of the Trinity because the word *perichoreo*, which means "to encompass," is very much like the verb, *perichoreuo*, which means "to dance around." It conjures up a dynamic Trinitarian image of a divine round dance.

The concept of *perichoretic* movement suggests that the three distinct persons relate to one another in a movement of equal relations. Johnson states, "Divine life circulates without any anteriority or posteriority, with-out any superiority or inferiority of one to the other."[8] With this in mind, each theologian's description of the Trinity will be presented.

---

6. Soskice argues that "God in the Trinity is not a lonely father who is aloof, above and indifferent. Rather, this God is the one who is 'with us' and who is fully present to our human history—even to the point of taking human flesh and dying on the cross—and fully present to us now in the Spirit." To confess God as triune is to bear witness to the fact that God has met us in particular moments, in particular ways. "To call upon the triune God is an act of faith. It reveals our conviction that God has acted, and does act, in concrete moments of history Soskice, "Trinity and Feminism," 139–45.

7. LaCugna, *God for Us*, 271.

8. Johnson, *She Who Is*, 220.

Catherine LaCugna

In *God for Us: The Trinity and Christian Life,* Catherine LaCugna asserts that the doctrine of the Trinity expresses the idea that God is *with us.* God, as revealed in the covenant with Israel, in the incarnation of Jesus Christ and in the gift of the Holy Spirit, is God as God who is not "within itself" but rather a person (God) turned toward others in love. In Trinitarian theology the essence of God is to be in relationship to other persons. For LaCugna, the Triune God is communal as well as personal. Throughout her work, LaCugna highlights the Cappadocian use of the term "person" as a relational term (understood as "being toward another"). Following the Cappadocians, LaCugna claims that relationality and mutuality are the very characters of God. "God's To-Be is To-Be-in-relationship, and God's being-in-relationship-to-us *is* what God is."[9]

In addition to her emphasis on relationship as the meaning of the Triune God, she deepens the understanding of human beings' call to live as the Trinity does. LaCugna suggests that humans are created in the image of God as relational; humans are created to live in communion. Living Trinitarian faith requires living out of God's life for and with us. In this sense, the Trinity can be used as a model for human relationships.[10] As God exists in relation, human beings exist in relation with God, other human beings and the world. Without others, persons would not exist. LaCugna's Trinitarian ontology of relationality is the essence not only for God, but also for human relationship. LaCugna writes: "Living Trinitarian faith means living God's life: living from and for God, from and for others . . . Living Trinitarian faith means living together in harmony and communion with every other creature in the common household of God . . . Living Trinitarian faith means adhering to the gospel of liberation from sin and fractured relationship."[11]

To follow God is to live in communion with God, one another and all creation. LaCugna's insight is that Trinitarian theology can be described as a "theology of relationship." She describes this divine life as a *"perichoretic outpouring of love."* Living Trinitarian faith means living God's life: living God's life with one another.

---

9. LaCugna, *God for Us,* 250.

10. Ibid., 378.

11. Ibid., 401.

Karen Baker-Fletcher

Karen Baker-Fletcher begins with this question: If God provides for the well-being of all creation, then why is there evil in the world and why is there so much suffering?

Baker-Fletcher examines the nature of God in relation to creation and in response to the suffering in the world. She views this violence against creation as "sin." Sin violates both God and creation; the consequences of sin and evil are *han* and blues. Borrowing Andrew Sung Park's concept of *han*, Baker-Fletcher says that *han* in Korean culture shares some common ground with the African American cultural understanding of the blues as the universal experience of human pain and suffering in the diverse cultural forms.[12] The world seems to be filled with the fullness of *han* and blues.

The question then becomes, who is God, and what is God doing in the world of *han* and blues? In response to this theodicy question, Baker-Fletcher discusses the Trinity. God is a relationship of three modes of being, in dynamic movement. All three persons of the Trinity have a common work of love, creativity, justice, righteousness, goodness, and power, yet they are distinct. Baker-Fletcher describes the work of the Trinity as *divine dancing*—"God's dance within the divine community."[13]

What does it mean to dance with God? To dance with the divine is to dance with courage. Human beings need courage to dance with God and others to participate in God's aim for the well-being of creation in spite of the problem of evil.[14] God wants people to find a new kind of courage, "to stop playing with evil and to start working with God, to start being a healed and whole creation." We can choose to live into goodness or evil. God does not make every decision for us, but rather all creation responsively participates in moments of decision in which each individual has agency and power. God partially determines creation, but not absolutely.[15] She writes, "The emphasis of my own womanist work is that even when God does not liberate us in the time or way that we want, God encourages us to continue struggling for healing and wholeness from hatred and violence."[16]

---

12. Baker-Fletcher, *Dancing with God,* 97.

13. Ibid., 63.

14. Ibid., 73–74.

15. Ibid., 80.

16. Ibid., x–xi.

Baker-Fletcher emphasizes that human suffering does not have the last word. We are not alone when we suffer, because the Trinity is with us, leading us toward redemptive overcoming of evil. Women have fought to change rape and domestic violence laws, seeking justice. These are people who do not simply bear their crosses. They pick up these crosses to overcome suffering. They actively seek to end suffering and violence, refusing to acquiesce to evil.[17]

In summary, the Triune God is dancing. Healing and resurrection power are the particular characteristics of the divine dance. All three relational actions create, recreate, and renew. It is "a healing dance of the Trinity." The Holy Spirit encourages the dance of Triune God, calling all to participate in the dance of divine love, creativity, healing, justice, and renewal. The Holy Spirit creates beauty out of ugliness, celebrates life in the midst of suffering, and walks in love in the midst of hate.[18] The dancing Trinity brings healing to people who suffer and urges human beings to participate in this divine healing dance through resistance and hope. As Fletcher-Baker says, "In the beginning, there was dance."[19]

Elizabeth Johnson

Elizabeth Jonson asks, "How does one see the living God through one's experience of suffering?" Trinitarian language, for Johnson, is an interpretation of who God is in the midst of suffering. Johnson tries to retrieve the symbol of God as Trinity to enable it to function in ways that are redemptive, especially to/for women.

Johnson's contributions, in terms of Trinitarian language, are first of all, that she provides a new frame to see God as Sophia; she changes the pronoun, which refers to God, from "He" to "She"; and she reorders the classic Trinity of Father—Son—Holy Spirit to Spirit—Jesus—Mother. By placing the Spirit as the starting point of her Trinitarian theology, Johnson seeks to address the neglect of pneumatology within Western theology. The marginalized Spirit becomes the first. By doing so, Johnson develops the Triune God with a female image named Holy Wisdom/Sophia, under the titles Spirit-Sophia, Jesus-Sophia, and Mother-Sophia. The movement into this Trinitarian proposal is from Spirit-Sophia, the Giver of life, who

17. Ibid., 150–52.
18. Ibid., 146.
19. Ibid., 160.

renews, Jesus-Sophia, who becomes enfleshed in Jesus, and to the ultimate Source of our origin, Mother-Sophia. For her, the Trinity is like a "three-foldness of relation."[20]

In this Trinitarian discourse, Johnson places suffering at the center.[21] She argues that a theology of God needs to take into account the suffering in the world. The symbol of the suffering God signals that the mystery of God is present in solidarity with those who suffer. She shows that God who suffers is also revealed by Jesus-Sophia, the crucified one, love poured out, and by Spirit-Sophia, "crying, admonishing, sorrowing, weeping, rejoicing, groaning, comforting."[22]

The mystery of the Triune God is in the world in solidarity with those who suffer. In the midst of suffering, the presence of divine compassion transforms suffering, not mitigating its evil but bringing an incomprehensible consolation and comfort. The image of the powerless suffering of God might be dangerous for some women in some situations. How, then, can a suffering God be helpful to women?

Johnson says that speaking about God's suffering can help by strengthening human responsibility. Knowing that we are not abandoned makes all the difference. To say this, for Johnson, is not to rationalize or valorize suffering. It points to the real mystery of the Trinitarian God as an ally against suffering and transforms the community for the practice of love and justice that corresponds to this mystery.

Knowing God is impossible unless we enter into a life of love and communion with others. Attending to women's experience of suffering and response to suffering can shape language about God that makes divine mystery more religiously accessible in the midst of disaster. Therefore, the point of speaking of the suffering God is that "it facilitates the praxis of hope."[23] Thus, speaking about the suffering God can bring resistance to women's suffering. Johnson notes, "Light dawns, courage is renewed, tears are wiped away, a new moment of life arises. Toward that end, speaking about suffering Sophia-God of powerful compassionate love serves as an ally of resistance and a wellspring of hope."[24]

20. Johnson, *She Who Is*, 216.

21. See ibid., ch. 12.

22. Ibid., 266.

23. Ibid., 217.

24. Ibid., 272.

The Main Functions of the Trinity

I have discussed three feminist theologians' understanding of the Trinity. LaCugna, Baker-Fletcher, and Johnson have showed some common ground in their Trinity. First, their notion of the Trinity is parallel with the *perichoretic* dynamics. Second, they agree that the Triune God, who is relational, empathically responds to human suffering. Finally, the Trinity requires human actions toward injustice and violence and brings resistance and hope. Therefore, according to them, Trinitarian theology emphasizes human participation and cooperation with the work of the Trinity. We recognize ourselves to be not only recipients but also participants in the work of God. As God is with us, so we are called to be with one another. Based on those reflections, I suggest two functions of the Trinity: 1) Make God and the creation dance; 2) *Salim*: make life new.

Make God Dance; Make the Creation Dance

The three theologians above all talk of *perichoresis* when regarding the Trinity. With this metaphor, the Trinity dances and inspires the whole creation to dance. I want to add the Korean concepts of *han* and *jeong* to this image.

Baker-Fletcher's "dance" and "dancing Trinity" are metaphors that refer to the dynamic and ongoing movement of God in creation as God continuously creates and recreates. In *perichoresis*, the three modes of being dynamically and relationally dance around and within one another.

God, who is Spirit, moves in the world in *perichoresis*—a type of sacred dance, a movement in and through creation. In other words, God as Trinity changes and is not static. The dance does not stay where we think it should stay. The dancing Trinity is not just one and not just three. It keeps moving, slides freely and goes beyond our expectation.

Since the cross often brings issues to abused women related to their suffering, I want to see the cross event in relation to the dance metaphor. The cross was not only the place where Jesus suffered and died but where the Trinity danced around. In addition, I want to emphasize that the cross is also where *han* and *jeong* of the divinity danced; it was where the dynamic movement of the Trinity is embodied with sorrow and hope.

Han is the wound in the heart—heart-woundedness. Andrew Sung Park says, "God's *han*, the wounded heart of God, is exposed on the cross."[25]

---

25. Park, *Wounded Heart of God*, 121.

Han is not only the "abysmal" experience of pain; it is also feelings of abandonment and helplessness. Park indicates that sin not only hurts humanity but also God; it becomes a wound for God. God is in solidarity with humanity and thus open to being wounded. God's love for humanity suffers on the cross.

Not only *han* but *jeong* is embodied on the cross, according to Anne Joh. By arguing we need more creative ways of imagining the divine, Joh asserts that the symbol of the cross performs a double gesture and requires a double reading. The cross embodies Jesus's embodiment of *han*/abjection and his radical *jeong* for us.[26]

As the life force of Korean people, *jeong* is rooted in relationality. Korean people describe one aspect of this connected relationality of life, *jeong*, as "sticky." I assume that Jesus might have felt the stickiness of love and hate toward humanity at the cross. His willingness to suffer was possible only because he had *jeong* for us.

Another aspect of *jeong* is that it is transgressive. *Jeong* works powerfully to blur the boundary. *Jeong* moves freely and has the capacity to transgress across diverse borders and boundaries.[27] Therefore, Joh argues that *jeong* has power to unravel *han* through heart-connectedness; *jeong* may overcome *han* through the redemptive work of love. In other words, *jeong* is needed to bring wholeness and healing from *han*. Joh states, "What is significant about the cross is not that Jesus died on it but that because of his living out of *jeong*, he ends up de facto on the cross."[28] God and humanity become interconnected through *jeong*.

The cross is the site where death and life coexist. It was where the Trinity danced around—the dance of God, Jesus and the Spirit; the dance of death and resurrection; the dance of sorrow and hope. *Han* and *jeong* of the Trinity danced around.

The power of the dancing Trinity is that it is not the Trinity alone who dances; the dancing Trinity invites the whole creation to dance; human beings are also called to participate in response to the struggle between good and evil. As evil changes its face, the dance of life changes its movement to respond. With each moment, the steps may be "slower or faster, simpler or

---

26. Joh, *Heart of the Cross*, 87.

27. Ibid., 153.

28. Ibid., 106.

more complicated, but always fluid."[29] God calls us to live the dance in all its dynamic, just, and liberating power.

The Trinity dances. It is about God's courageous, gracious, relational, Trinitarian response to the entire earth. Because the dance is not static, people are not locked in the past. They move forward and backward. The dance potentially transforms one's experiences into new becoming when one chooses not to repeat the suffering of one's past. As Baker-Fletcher puts it, "The particular dance of faith seeking understanding presented here is a liberating dance in a world of crucifixion. It is intertwined with dances of survival and transcendence . . . It is a dance of life. It defies the dance of the walking dead."[30]

In the midst of suffering, women can dance. Through the dynamic of dance, women can lament and mourn, yet dare to hope. It may move some from suffering to healing, from *han* into *jeong*. To dance with the Trinity is to dance with courage. Calls to accountability continue the work of the Trinity. Therefore, we women can dance with the Trinity—with courage and hope, having *han* and *jeong* in our hearts; people's *han* and *jeong*, hope and sorrow, dance. The issue of the cross is not a matter of 'bearing one's cross" but rather a matter of using the meaning of the cross for Christian women for a liberation, change, and resurrection.

Crucifixion and resurrection are common in everyday life. The dance of the Trinity helps us to keep hoping in the midst of suffering, transforms our cries into laughs, wounds into healing, *han* into *jeong*. As a matter of fact, suffering may not necessarily be transformed. All aspects of our life will be present in the dance: suffering and hope, *han* and *jeong*, good and bad. It is about dance. All things come and go around. When we acknowledge this, it will make our life humble and hopeful. Life is a circle of suffering and hope. We have to acknowledge the suffering in our own lives, but because of *jeong*, we do not give up. We continue to strive, to seek healing and hope for a better tomorrow.

Salim: Make Life New

The dance of the Trinity is a dance of *han* and *jeong*. The Trinity makes the creation dance. What else can the Trinity do to help respond to people's

---

29. Baker-Fletcher, *Dancing with God*, 46–47.
30. Ibid., 48.

suffering? If there is another job of the Trinity, I would say *salim*: Trinity does *salim*.

In *She Who Is*, Johnson says that divine power is "vitality, an empowering vigor that reaches out and awakens freedom and strength in oneself and others. It is an energy that brings forth, stirs up, and fosters life, enabling autonomy and friendship. It is a movement of spirit that builds, mends, struggles with and against, celebrates and laments. It transforms people, and bonds them with one another and to the world."[31] Johnson says that the symbol of the suffering God releases its empowering vitality. Koreans have a word with a similar meaning: *salim*.

Salim, in general, is used to refer to Korean women's everyday household chores such as cooking, cleaning, etc. This involves the common and everyday things that women do to make life possible and comfortable for their families and others.

Regardless of the ceaseless amount of work for the common good of families and communities, women's housework, *salim*, has been underestimated as if it is "nothing" or not important in a patriarchal society. When asked "What do you do for a living," many Korean women would say, "Nothing. I just do *salim* in my house," which means "I am a housewife."

The noun *salim*, generally meaning women's "house chores," originally came from the verb *salida*, which means "making things alive," "giving life." However, most Korean people, still now, would not link these two words to a same root. For many Koreans, *salim* means just "house chores" and is not related to "life." However, in the late 1990's, in academia, the word for the women's house chores, *salim*, got a new interpretation from scholars. It was Jiha Kim, a Korean male poet, who gave attention and articulated the meaning of *salim* in relation to the verb, *salida*—giving life. He drew the meaning of the word *salim* out of women's house chores and broadened it into the public space through declaring a "*salim* movement" for women and men. Kim defines the *salim* movement as a life movement including the ordinary actions that create a responsible society for the realization of one's inner life or original life that continues along with the flow of life.[32]

Having been inspired by Kim, some theologians use the term *salim* in their theology. JungBae Lee suggests church could be a "*salim* community," which means the community in which church members participate

---

31. Johnson, *She Who Is*, 270.

32. Kim, *Saengmyungkwa Jachi*.

is a *salim* movement in their daily lives.[33] A Korean feminist theologian, HyunKyung Chung, coined a word, *salimist,* Korean women who are doing *salim* for the family and the society. Chung defines *salimist* as a "Korean ecofeminist or anyone who wants to share the vision of a Korean eco feminist." *Salimists* make things alive, embrace and recycle everybody and everything.

SeongHee Kim uses "*salim* hermeneutics" for Korean women's biblical interpretation as a way of engaging ordinary Korean women's reading of the Bible and actualizing the meaning of the Bible in Korean women's *salim* practice. *Salim* hermeneutics seeks "to give life and meaning to ordinary tasks, to restore broken things, to make peace, to ensure justice, and to participate in the new creation of God for living together."[34]

Based on his eleven years' contact in Korea and with Korean people, James Poling suggests *han, jeong,* and *salim* as three Korean concepts that can contribute to American pastoral theology. While the concepts of *han* and *jeong* are becoming familiar to American theology, Poling adds *salim* as a resource that can be used for American theology. Poling finds the strengths of these three Korean virtues in their multiplicity and ambiguity; always contestable, richer than their description and beyond their definitions.[35]

Salim, with its new interpretation, means, "making things alive" and "giving life." Indeed, women's *salim* includes giving things life, healing wounds, mending broken things, and creating new environments for life of all creation. I suggest that the persons of the Trinity are engaged in *salim* as an internal dynamic and in relation to the world. I propose the phrase, *Salim* Trinity.

Chung suggests that anyone who wants to share the vision of a Korean ecofeminist is a *salimist.* In addition, I propose that the Spirit is also a *salimist.* Chung writes: "A *Salimist* has perfected the skill or art of making things alive, e.g., feeding everybody so that they are all full and happy, creating peace, health, and abundant living for the family (the very large extended family of all forms of life) and a beautiful living environment. Also, a *Salimist* touches everything like a magician, a revolutionary or a God/ess. At her touch, everything starts to smile, grow, and become vivid,

---

33. Lee, *Hangukjeok Saengmyung Shinhak.*

34. Kim, "Reading the Bible from the Perspective of Korean Women," 102–3.

35. Poling, "Is There a Korean Contribution to U.S. Pastoral Theology?"

colorful, and alive. She has a vision for fundamental social change, gets involved in movements, and develops strategies."[36]

The Trinity is *salimist*, indeed: mending broken hearts, giving life, recycling everything, helping people love and not harm one another, and working for a better community. This is the cooperative work of the Trinity and women who do *salim*.

Chung told a story about an extraordinary experience during a time of meditation:

> During my meditation, I see myself arriving at a temple riding on a dragon. I went to the place where "She" always is—where I used to come and cry. She always listened to me and gave me a warm meal. I tried to find her. "Mother!" I cried, but "She" is not here today. Being tired of waiting for her, I decided to help with her house chores. I watered the plants and prepared dinner in the kitchen. Someone came. It was not "her" but a little child who seemed about three years old. The child said, "Mother! I am hungry" and hugged me. I washed the little child's face and hands and prepared a meal for the child. "You better eat slowly," I said. I gave the child a cup of water. While the child was eating rice, I found a mirror nearby. When I looked in the mirror, the person in the mirror was "She"—not me. She smiled at me. "Mum, I am hungry. Give me more!" said the child. I gave the child more rice. Tears were rolling down my face.[37]

This is a moment of *salim* through the Spirit. We don't know which one received new life energy through this *salim* moment—whether "She," "Chung," or "the child"—or maybe all three of them. That is the mystery of the work of divinity. It is the Spirit who does *salim* and dances through us.

Reflections with Abused Women

Having explored the meaning of the Trinity in relation to suffering, presented by three feminist theologians, I come to the question of suffering again. Many Christian women have heard pastors say that their suffering has some purpose—for example, suffering builds one's character or is a test of one's faith. Marie Fortune suggests that this Christian teaching is a

---

36. Chung, "Salimist Manifesto," 237.

37. Translated by HeeSun Kim from Chung, *Kyulkukeun Arumdaumi Urirul Kuwonhalkkuya*, 96–97.

"doormat theology" which encourages victims' to blame themselves or God for the suffering they experience. Self-blame or God-blame for one's suffering simply avoids acknowledging that a particular person is responsible for the abusive acts.[38]

Fortune says that personal violence presents a victim with two options: endurance or transformation. Endurance means remaining a victim; transformation means becoming a survivor.[39] She claims, "The question for us is not who sinned or how God can allow women to be beaten and raped, but how can we allow this to go unchallenged? Who is accountable for this suffering and how can justice be wrought here? "[40] The questions of suffering should be changed; the real question is not, "Why?" but, "What do people do with that suffering?"

> One week after the first call, I got a call from the same woman who asked if she needed to bear her cross. At the time, I was in the beginning process of research about the Trinity related to women's suffering so I wanted to see whether my thinking about the Trinity could help her. It might be a little bit early, but I wanted to suggest a different angle for her to understand her suffering. When she mentioned again about bearing her cross as Jesus did, I asked her, "Was he alone when he suffered? And did he just die on the cross?" She responded, "No, he was not alone according to the Bible and he resurrected from the dead." Then, I asked her if she wanted to follow Jesus. She was silent for a few minutes. I asked her again carefully "what if the Trinity was with you through your suffering and your resurrection." Another few minutes of silence, and then she said, "Resurrection . . . why didn't I think of resurrection?" Then, she said, "Um . . . I feel like now I have more listeners and supporters when I pray if I think of the Trinity. From now on, I will think about the meaning of Jesus' resurrection and what my resurrection will be. I hope the Holy Spirit can help me." I said I would pray for her that the Holy Spirit can guide and support her to find a way out of her suffering.

I don't know what decision she made after the conversation, but I hope, at least, that she will be reminded of resurrection whenever she looks up at the cross. And maybe she will not think of Jesus only anymore but also think of the Holy Spirit.

38. Adams and Fortune, eds., *Violence against Women and Children*, 89.

39. Ibid., 90.

40. Ibid., 88.

The Christian church should articulate a theology of empowerment rather than a theology of passive endurance since Jesus did not come to the world to suffer and die but, I believe, to proclaim good news to the poor and the oppressed.

The Triune God is present in the midst of suffering and the Trinity gives us the strength and courage to resist injustice and to transform suffering. It is grounded in the conviction of hope and empowered by a passion for justice. Christian women should resist their unjust suffering. By refusing to endure and by seeking to transform suffering, we join God's work of making justice and healing brokenness. The Christian church should encourage a faith that provides women with resources for strength and transformation rather than resources for endurance.

In summary, tragically, suffering is somehow inevitable in this world, but new life is always happening. The moving part for me is, as Catherine Keller puts it, "This may only be possible because Job refused to suppress piously the turbulent truth of his own experience, but has grieved and raged and confronted the meaning of life."[41]

Johnson describes the name of the Trinity as one name in three inflections. To say that the Trinity is one name in three inflections is to identify three different tones that sing of this truth, three different grammars by which it is spoken.[42] The Triune God has different, at least three, modes of responding to human suffering.

Pui-lan Kwok gives an interesting anecdote about listening to a performance of Osvaldo Golijov's *La Pasión según San Marcos*. She writes that it "is sung and performed in Spanish, the piece that combined voice, strings, and brass, drums and percussion, and Afro-Cuban dance. What is most iconoclastic and nonconventional about the work is that the roles of Jesus, Pilate, Peter, and the people were sung by the soloists, and the chorus without regard to numbers and to gender. Thus, Jesus was sometimes a woman, sometimes a man, a group of voices, and a dancer."[43]

I imagine this multidynamic movement can echo the experience of many Christian women who suffer. At least one of those tones can resonate with one woman's suffering, can console and bring her hope. The next time, other tones/relations/voices/persons can meet her in an unexpected

41. Catherine Keller, *On the Mystery*, 76.

42. Johnson, *Quest for the Living God*, 216.

43. Kwok, *Postcolonial Imagination and Feminist Theology*, 185. Osvaldo Golijov, *La Pasión según San Marcos* (*Saint Mark Passion*).

time and space. In other words, "it" is not static and is always changing. However, if "it" is there for us, dancing, coming to our bodies, making us new, if "She" empowers us for resistance and makes us dream for a different future, then "it," "the Divinity," or "She" is that which we can embrace during our suffering, whether or not it is classically called "Trinity." "It" is the divinity who speaks to my heart. I give the Trinity freedom not to be confined to human language, numbers, and descriptions. There are various ways the Trinity understands and responds to women's suffering. God the Trinity knows/feels women's *han*; She has *jeong* toward human beings who are capable of doing both evil and justice; they do *salim* for the well-being of the creation. With a new connotation, now I believe in the Trinity. She is a *Salimist* who has unfathomable love for the whole creation—including you and me.

Epilogue

SOUTH KOREAN ECONOMIC AND cultural power has exploded on the global stage in the last one hundred years. A small, relatively obscure country in Asia has become the thirteenth largest economy with one of the most vibrant missionary Christian churches that has ever existed. This has happened in spite of the severe trauma of twentieth-century colonization, world war, civil war, and transformation by modernist global forces. The South Korean people carry the scars, the *han*, of these events, and yet they have emerged as a world force. Both the trauma and the transformation have happened during the growth of Western, Protestant Christianity. What factors account for this recent transformation, and what does it contribute to the world culture?

Some scholars attribute the transformation of South Korea to the influence of modern ideas in collaboration with Christian missionary movements. They say that Christianity brought values and practices that enabled the Korean people to develop their God-given potential. What is possible for South Korea is possible for many other nations of the world. Other scholars attribute the transformation of South Korea to the deeply held ancient values of traditional Asian religions, including Shamanism, Buddhism, Taoism, and Confucianism. They say that Christianity and modernism are thin layers that merely provide access to global culture and markets, but the real contribution of South Korean people and institutions comes because of their identity as Koreans.

In this book, we entertained a third idea that the South Korean transformation is the result of a unique interreligious confluence that enables South Korea to embrace the ambiguity and multiplicity of many religions, values, ideologies, and values. For centuries, Korea has engaged in an experiment in interreligious life, as one world religion after another has struggled for dominance and then taken its place within the multiplicity that has emerged. Perhaps South Korea is an example of a postmodern culture, one in which the forces of domination have subsided and a new culture of cooperation between competing ideologies has become possible. If South Korea is a genuine postmodern culture, perhaps it has a contribution to make to other nations and cultures that continue to believe that one ideology must dominate all others in order to have a national identity at all.

In this book project, we have been particularly interested in the South Korean contributions to pastoral theology, that is, the healing practices for individuals, families, communities, and nations. The urgency of finding healing narratives and practices is self-evident in a world characterized by interpersonal violence, cultural domination, wars between nations and religions, and the threat of ecological catastrophe. Pastoral theologians are Christian practitioners who focus every day on how to help people recover from the wounds of everyday life within modern culture. How do persons survive the many threats to their health and salvation when conflict, violence, and danger face them on every side? How do people survive jobs that destroy their autonomy and dignity? How do people survive unemployment and poverty during times of economic depression and shifting global markets? How do people manage their roles as marriage partners, parents, and Christian believers when their communities and environment are destroyed by corporations seeking profit? These are the questions of pastoral theology.

Within South Korean Christian churches, there has been an explosion of ministries of pastoral care and counseling in recent decades. Every family has its own story of trauma to tell, and many people seek understanding of how they can find healing for their trauma. In situations of trauma, people seek religious answers to why things have happened as they have, and what resources will bring the possibility of surviving and thriving again.

Within the interreligious context of South Korea, we have discovered helpful connections between Western feminist interpretations of the Trinity in Christian theology and concepts such as *han, jeong,* and *salim.* In theology, the Trinity has become, for some scholars, a concept about human relationality and generativity within the doctrine of God and between God and the creation. Given the character of God as relational, the implication is that the image of God in human beings is relational. That is, we discover our truest identity when we understand ourselves in relation to self, others, and God. Just as the Trinity is characterized by respect, equality, and creativity, so human beings are called to relationships of respect, equality, and creativity. We discovered in this project that the relationality of God and humans in community is crucial for healing and human thriving, and that relationality has its roots in religion, especially in interreligious contexts.

South Korean Christians know something about living in relationships that are characterized by ambiguity and multiplicity. *Han* describes the interreligious reality of shared suffering and trauma that can lead to depression, suicide, murder, and revenge, or it can lead to solidarity and commitment to seek justice in community. *Jeong* describes the deep emotional bonding that occurs among humans when they live together and share common challenges. *Jeong* is "sticky," because once persons are bonded by *jeong*, they belong to one another for good or evil. *Salim* is a concept that emphasizes the everyday labor involved in fostering healthy and sustaining relationships in which we give and receive life with one another. In a modern culture of individualism and competition, *salim* has often been devalued because it does not contribute to the goals of selfish attainment at the expense of others. But *salim* potentially helps us return to the reality God creates for human life: our relationships with self, others, and God. What has been devalued within modern culture turns out to be the bedrock of human life and love.

For Christians, Jesus Christ is the ideal human being and the one who reveals the character of God. In this book, we have asked about the revelation of Christ from two cultures. Through our work together our faith in Jesus Christ has been confirmed. Jesus was a person who was fully relational, who cared about the people he lived with and encountered, and who sought their healing and salvation. In Jesus we see the depth of God's love, even God's suffering, with humanity in its beautiful and tragic existence. In Jesus, we see *jeong*, his love for all the world; we see *han*, his suffering and resilience on the cross; we see *salim*, his ministries of peace and life giving to celebrate the full reality of the beloved community.

We hope that *salim*, through the dance of *han* and *jeong* for love and justice, will bring healing and wholeness to our everyday lives. Do you feel Jesus's *jeong* toward humanity? Do you feel *jeong* toward the Korean people? Welcome to the dance of *han*, sticky *jeong*, and *salim*.

Glossary of Cited Korean Words

Baekje: An ancient kingdom centered in southwest Korea

Chondogyo: The first of late nineteenth-century religious groups that draw on interreligious resources from Asian religions

Dangun: The legendary founder of Korean culture in 2333 BCE

Donghak: A nineteenth-century religious and political reform movement

Goryeo: A Korean dynasty that ruled from the tenth to the fourteenth century, with its capital in Kaesong

Goguryeo: An ancient kingdom in northern Korea and Manchuria

GoJoseon: Ancient Korea before 57 BCE

Gut: A shamanistic ritual of chanting, dancing, and communicating with spirits

Halmani: An older woman

Han: Intergenerational suffering and oppression

Hananim: The most high God, adopted by Protestant Christians as the common name for monotheistic deity.

Jeong: attachment, love, emotional tie

Joseon (Chosen): The Korean dynasty from the fourteenth to the twentieth century, with capital in Seoul

Juche: Self-reliance or independence, adopted as a central concept by Kim IlSung in North Korea.

Minjok: The ethnic and racial identity of Korean people

Minjung: "Many people," used by Minjung theology to refer to the poor, the oppressed

Mudang: Female Korean shaman

Mugyo: Korean Shamanism

Nei, Wai: Inside, outside, respectively; from Confucian influence, usually means "inside the house" and "outside the house" to describe the gender roles of men and women.

Ren: Central Confucian concept meaning "love," "benevolence," "being human."

Salim: Making life, making peace

Silhak: An eighteenth-century reform movement arising from Christian influences

Silla: The ancient kingdom centered in southeastern Korea; and Korean dynasty from first to tenth century, with its capital in Gyeongju

Wu Wei: The concept of receptivity from Taoism

Bibliography

Adams, Carol J., and Marie M. Fortune, editors. *Violence against Women and Children: A Christian Theological Sourcebook*. New York: Continuum, 1995.

Ahn, Byung-Mu. *Jesus of Galilee*. Hong Kong: The Christian Conference of Asia, 2004.

Baker, Don. "Hananim, Hanøunim, Hanullim, and Hanøollim: The Construction of Terminology for Korean Monotheism." *The Review of Korean Studies*. Seoul: The Academy of Korean Studies 5/1 (2002) 105–31.

———. *Korean Spirituality*. Dimensions of Asian Spirituality. Honolulu: University of Hawaii Press, 2008.

Baker-Fletcher, Karen. *Dancing with God: The Trinity from a Womanist Perspective*. St. Louis: Chalice, 2006.

Berinyuu, Abraham Adu. *Towards Theory and Practice of Pastoral Counseling in Africa*. European University Studies. Series 27, Asian and African Studies 25. London: Lang, 1989.

Booth, Wayne C. et al. *The Craft of Research*. Chicago Guides to Writing, Editing, and Publishing. Chicago: University of Chicago Press, 1995.

Brandt, Vincent S. R. *A Korean Village: Between Farm and Sea*. Harvard East Asian Series 65. Cambridge: Harvard University Press, 1971.

Brown, George Thompson. *Mission to Korea*. Seoul: The Presbyterian Church of Korea, 1962.

Brown, Joanne Carlson, and Carole R. Bohn, editors. *Christianity, Patriarchy, and Abuse: A Feminist Critique*. New York: Pilgrim, 1989.

Brown, Karen McCarthy. *Mama Lola: A Vodou Priestess in Brooklyn*. Updated and expanded edition. Comparative Studies in Religion and Society 4. Berkeley: University of California Press, 2001.

Buswell, Robert E., editor. *Religions of Korea in Practice*. Princeton Readings in Religions. Princeton: Princeton University Press, 2007.

Buswell, Robert E. Jr., and Timothy S. Lee, editors. *Christianity in Korea*. Honolulu: University of Hawaii Press, 2006.

Caputo, John. *Deconstruction in a Nutshell: A Conversation with Jacques Derrida*. New York: Perspectives in Continental Philosophy 1. Fordham University Press, 1996.

Chang, Ul-Byong. "Shin Chaeho's Nationalism and Anarchism." *Korea Journal* 26/11 (1986) 21–40.

Choe Sang-Hun. "Foreign Brides Challenge South Korean Prejudices." *New York Times*, June 24, 2005. Online: http://www.nytimes.com/2005/06/23/world/asia/23iht-brides.html?scp=1&sq=Foreign%20Brides%20Challenge&st=cse/.

———. "South Korea Offers Food Aid to North." *New York Times*, October 26, 2009. Online: http://www.nytimes.com/2009/10/27/world/asia/27korea.html/.

Choi, Joon-sik. *Folk-Religion: The Customs in Korea*. Spirit of Korean Cultural Roots. Seoul: Ewha Womans University Press, 2005.

———. *Hankuk Jonggyosa Baro Bogi* [Understanding the History of Korean Religion]. Seoul: Hanwul, 2007.

———. *Understanding Koreans and Their Culture*. Albany, NY: Her One Media, 2007.

Chung, HeeSung. "Ilbonkun Wianbueui Doktukhan Hananim Imiji Yungu." ["God-Representation and the Sex-Slave of World War II."] *Jongkoyunku* [*Religious Studies*] 47 (2007) 225–51.

———. "Kundaehankukyusungeud Mosung Kyunghumkwa Minjok." ["Motherhood and Nation in the Christianity of Modern Korea."] In *Minjuokwa Yousungsinhak* [*Nations and Feminist Theology*], edited by Hankukyusungsinhakhoe [the Korean Association of Feminist Theology], 255–83. Seoul: Handul, 2006.

———. "Divorce Counseling with Korean Women in the Court." *Journal of Ministry and Counseling* (2006) 8.

———. "Pastoral Theological Understanding of the Sexually Abused." *Korean Journal of Christian Studies* (2006) 43.

Chung, Hyun Kyung. *Struggle to Be the Sun Again: Introducing Asian Women's Theology*. Maryknoll, NY: Orbis,1990.

———. *Kyulkukeun Arumdaumi Urirul Kuwonhalkkuya* [*In the End, the Beauty Will Save Us All*]. Pa-Ju: Yolimwon, 2001.

———. *Goddess-Spell according to HyunKyung*. Pa-Ju: Yolimwon, 2001.

Chung, Sung-Kuh. *Church Growth and Preaching: A Historical Study of Preaching in the Korean Church*. Bangalore: Center for Contemporary Christianity, 2007.

CIA World Factbook, 2008, online https://www.cia.gov/library/publications/the-world-factbook/print/ks.html.

Clark, Donald N. *Living Dangerously in Korea: The Western Experience,1900–1950*. The Missionary Enterprise in Asia. Norwalk, CT: Eastbridge, 2003.

Clinebell, Howard. *Ecotherapy: Healing Ourselves, Healing the Earth*. Minneapolis: Fortress, 1996.

Cobb, John B. Jr. *The Earthist Challenge to Economism: A Theological Critique of the World Bank*. New York: St. Martin's, 1999.

Commission on Theological Concerns of the Christian Conference of Asia, editor. *Minjung Theology: People as the Subjects of History*. London: Zed, 1981.

Confucius. *The Analects*. Penguin Classics. Harmondsworth: Penguin, 1979.

Cone, James. *God of the Oppressed*. Rev. ed. Maryknoll, NY: Orbis, 1997.

Cumings, Bruce. *Korea's Place in the Sun: A Modern History*. Updated ed. New York: Norton, 2005.

———. *North Korea: Another Country*. New York: New Press, 2004.

Daly, Mary. *Beyond God the Father*. Boston: Beacon, 1973.

Davie, Grace. *Europe: The Exceptional Case: Parameters of Faith in the Modern World*. Sarum Theological Lectures. London: Darton, Longman and Todd, 2002.

Deuchler, Martina. *The Confucian Transformation of Korea: A Study of Society and Ideology*. Harvard-Yenching Institute Monograph Series 36. Cambridge: Council on East Asian Studies, Harvard University, distributed by Harvard University Press, 1992.

Eckert, Carter J. et al. *Korea, Old and New: A History.* Seoul: Published for Harvard University by Ilchokak; distributed by Harvard University Press, 1990.

Feiser, James, and Bradley Dowden, general editors. *Internet Encyclopedia of Philosophy.* Online: http://www.iep.utm.edu/.

Focus on Korea: Korean History. Seoul: Seoul International Publishing House, 1986.

Golijov, Osvaldo, composer. *La Pasión según San Marcos.* María Guiand, conductor. Orquesta de Pasión. Scola Cantorum de Venezuela and soloists. Berlin: Deutche Gramaphon 4777461, 2010. 2 CDs.

Graham, Ella. *Dear Fannie Letters and Dear Home Folks Letters: 1907–1930.* Unpublished.

Graham, Larry. *Care of Persons, Care of Worlds: A Psychosystems Approach to Pastoral Care and Counseling.* Nashville: Abingdon, 1992.

Grayson, James Huntley. *Korea: A Religious History.* Oxford: Clarendon, 1989.

Grenz, Stanley. *A Primer on Postmodernism.* Grand Rapids: Eerdmans, 2008.

Griffin, David Ray. *Whitehead's Radically Different Postmodern Philosophy: An Argument for Its Contemporary Relevance.* SUNY Series in Philosophy. Albany: State University of New York Press, 2008.

Haggard, Stephan, and Marcus Noland. *Famine in North Korea: Markets, Aid, and Reform.* New York: Columbia University Press, 2007.

———. "Aid to North Korea," *KoreAm Journal* 18/8 (2007), no pages, Online: http://www.iie.com/publications/opeds/oped.cfm?ResearchID=797.

Hart, Dennis. *From Tradition to Consumption: Construction of a Capitalist Culture in South Korea.* Korean Studies Dissertation Series 2. Seoul: Jimoondang, 2001.

Hogarth, Hyun-key Kim. *Korean Shamanism and Cultural Nationalism.* Korean Studies Series 14. Seoul: Jimoondang, 1999.

"Horace Newton Allen." In *New World Encyclopedia,* Online: http://www.newworldencyclopedia.org/entry/Horace_Newton_Allen/.

Hurston, Zora Neale. *Tell My Horse: Voodoo and Life in Haiti and Jamaica.* Harper Perennial Modern Classics. New York: Harper Perennial, 2009.

Im Un-kil. "The Origin, Core Ideas, and Faith of Cheondo-gyo." In *Encounters: The New Religions of Korea and Christianity,* edited by Kim Sung-hae and James Heisig, 31–56. Seoul: The Royal Asiatic Society, 2008.

The Institute of Korean Church History Studies. *Han-guk Gidokgyo e Yeoksa II,* 285–381. Seoul: Gidokkyomunsa. [In English: "The Shinto Shrine Worship." In *A History of Korean Church,* 2:285–381. Seoul: The Christian Literature Press, 1990.]

Joe, Wanne J. *A Cultural History of Modern Korea: A History of Korean Civilization.* Edited with an introduction by Hongku A. Choe. Elizabeth, NJ: Hollym, 2001.

Joh, Wonhee Anne. *The Heart of the Cross: A Postcolonial Christology.* Louisville: Westminster John Knox, 2006.

Johnson, Elizabeth A. *She Who Is: The Mystery of God in Feminist Theological Discourse.* 10th anniversary edition. New York: Crossroad, 2002.

———. *Quest for the Living God: Mapping Frontiers in the Theology of God.* New York: Continuum: 2007.

"Joshu Washes the Bowl." In *The Gateless Gate,* by Huikai. Translated by Nyogen Senzaki and Saladin Reps. Los Angeles: Murray, 1934. Online: http://www.sacred-texts.com/bud/glg/glg07.htm/.

Kang, Namsoon. "Confucian Familism and Its Social/Religious Embodiment in Christianity: Reconsidering the Family Discourses from a Feminist Perspective." *Asia Journal of Theology* 18 (2004) 168–89.

Keller, Catherine. *On the Mystery: Discerning Divinity in Process.* Minneapolis: Fortress, 2008.

Keller, Nora Okja. *Comfort Woman: A Novel.* New York: Viking, 1997.

Kim, IlMyon. *Enno no guntai to Chosenjin ianfu* [*The Emperor's Army and the Korean Comfort Women*]. Tokyo: San'ichi Sobo, 1992.

Kim, In Soo. *Ju Gi-Cheul: The Life of the Reverend Soyang Ju Gi-Cheul, Lamb of Jesus.* Translated by Son Dal-Ig. Seoul: Presbyterian College and Theological Seminary Press, 2008.

Kim, Jiha. *Sang-myung-kwa Ja-chi* [*Life and Autonomy*]. Seoul: Sol Press, 1996.

Kim, Seong Hee. "Reading the Bible from the Perspective of Korean Women." Doing Theology from Korean's Women's Perspective: Toward Salim Hermeneutics. *EWHA Journal of Feminist Theology* 5 (2007) 93–116.

———. "Rupturing the Empire: Reading the Poor Widow as a Postcolonial Female Subject (Mark 12:41–44)." *Lectio Difficilior: European Electronic Journal for Feminist Exegesis* (January 2006) 1–21. Online: http://www.lectio.unibe.ch/06_1/PDF/kim_rupturing.pdf/.

Kim Sung-hae, and James Heisig, editors, *Encounters: The New Religions of Korea and Christianity.* Seoul: Royal Asiatic Society, 2008.

Kim, UnHey. "Women Leadership in the Korean Salimist Concept." In *Responsible Leadership: Global and Contextual Ethical Perspectives*, edited by Christoph Stuckelberger and J. N. K. Mugambi, 45–52. Globethics.net Series 1. Geneva: WCC Publications, 2007.

Ko, Dorothy et al., editors. *Women and Confucian Cultures in Premodern China, Korea, and Japan.* Berkeley: University of California Press, 2003.

Korean Council for Women Drafted for Military Sexual Slavery by Japan, compilers. Translated by Young Joo Lee. Edited by Keith Howard. *True Stories of the Korean Comfort Women.* London: Cassell, 1996.

"Korean Buddhism." In *New World Encyclopedia.* Online: http://www.newworldencyclopedia.org/entry/Korean_Buddhism/.

"Korean Music." Online: http://www.oocities.org/collegepark/theater/6580/music.html.tmp.

Kunuk, Zacharias, director. *The Fast Runner (Atanarjuat).* Montréal: Igloolik Isuma Productions Inc., 2000. DVD.

Kwok, Pui-lan. *Postcolonial Imagination and Feminist Theology.* Louisville: Westminster John Knox, 2005.

LaCugna, Catherine, *God for Us: The Trinity and Christian Life.* San Francisco: HarperSanFrancisco, 1991.

Lafayette Avenue Presbyterian Church. "The LAPC Story." Online: http://www.lapcbrooklyn.org/AboutLAPC2b.htm.

Lankov, Andre. "N. Korea Faces Unprecedented Food Crisis since 1990s." *Korea Times*, June 18, 2008. Online: http://koreatimes.co.kr/www/news/special/2011/04/180_26138.html

"Largest Cities of the World [2010]." *World Atlas.* Online: http://www.worldatlas.com/citypops.htm/.

Lausanne Theology Working Group, Africa Chapter. "A Statement on Prosperity Teaching." *Christianity Today*, December 8, 2009. Online: http://www.christianitytoday.com/ct/article_print.html?id=86009.

Lee, EunSun. "A Study of Korean Women's Spirituality within the Evolving Process of Korean Religious Culture Focused on Confucianism and Christianity." In *Sung/Sung/Sung eui Shinhak*. Seoul: Mosineunsaramdeul, 2011.

Lee JungBae. *Heankukjuk Sangmyung Shinhak [Korean Life Theology as the Systematic Theology]*. Seoul: Korean Methodist Seminary Press, 1996.

Lee, Jung Young. *The Trinity in Asian Perspective*. Nashville: Abingdon, 1996.

Lee, Ki-Baik. *A New History of Korea*. Translated by Edward W. Wagner with Edward J. Shultz. Cambridge: Harvard University Press, 1984.

Lee, Sang Oak. *Korean Language and Culture*. Seoul: Sotong, 2008.

"The Legend of Tan-Gun." *Life in Korea* (Website). Online: http://www.lifeinkorea.com/information/tangun.cfm.

Li, Chenyang, editor. *The Sage and the Second Sex: Confucianism, Ethics and Gender*. Chicago: Open Court, 2000.

Littlejohn, Ronnie. "Daoist Philosophy." In *Internet Encyclopedia of Philosophy*, edited by James Feiser and Bradley Dowden. Online: http://www.iep.utm.edu/daoism/.

———. "Laozi (Lao-tzu, fl. 6th c. BCE)." In *Internet Encyclopedia of Philosophy*, edited by James Feiser and Bradley Dowden. Online: http://www.iep.utm.edu/laozi/.

Lugo, Luis, and Brian Grim. "South Korea's Coming Election Highlights Christian Community." *Pew Forum on Religion & Public Life*, December 12, 2007. Online: http://pewresearch.org/pubs/657/south-koreas-coming-election-highlights-christian-community.

Lzu, Lao. *T'ai Shang Kan Ying P'ien*. Online: http://www.bessel.org/golden.

Mason, David A. *Spirit of the Mountains: Korea's San-Shin and Traditions of Mountain Worship*. Elizabeth, NJ: Hollym, 1999.

Mercadante, Susan. *Victims and Sinners: Spiritual Roots of Addiction and Recovery*. Louisville: Westminster John Knox, 1996.

Moltmann, Jürgen. *The Spirit of Life: A Universal Affirmation*. Translated by Margaret Kohl. Minneapolis: Fortress, 1992.

Nelson, Laura C. *Measured Excess: Status, Gender, and Consumer Nationalism in South Korea*. New York: Columbia University Press, 2000.

Oberdorfer, Don. *The Two Koreas: A Contemporary History*. New York: Basic Books, 2001.

Park, Andrew Sung. *From Hurt to Healing: A Theology of the Wounded*. Nashville: Abingdon Press, 2004.

———. *Triune Atonement: Christ's Healing for Sinners, Victims, and the Whole Creation*. Louisville: Westminster John Knox, 2009.

———. *The Wounded Heart of God: The Asian Concept of Han and the Christian Doctrine of Sin*. Nashville: Abingdon, 1993.

Park, Andrew Sung, and Susan L. Nelson, editors. *The Other Side of Sin: Woundedness from the Perspective of the Sinned-Against*. Albany: State University of New York, 2001.

Parsons, Susan Frank, editor. *The Cambridge Companion to Feminist Theology*. Cambridge Companions to Religion. Cambridge: Cambridge University Press, 2002.

Poling, James N. "Is There a Korean Contribution to US Pastoral Theology?" *Pastoral Psychology* 59/4 (2010) 1–12.

————. *Render unto God: Economic Vulnerability, Family Violence, and Pastoral Theology.* St. Louis: Chalice, 2002.

————. *Rethinking Faith: A Constructive Practical Theology.* Minneapolis: Fortress, 2011.

Poling, James N., and Lewis Mudge, editors. *Formation and Reflection: The Promise of Practical Theology.* Philadelphia: Fortress, 1987.

Rhodes, Harry A., editor. *History of the Korea Mission, Presbyterian Church USA.* Vol. 1, *1884–1934.* Seoul: The Presbyterian Church of Korea, 1934.

————, editor. *History of the Korea Mission, Presbyterian Church USA.* Vol. 2, *1935–1959,* Seoul: The Presbyterian Church of Korea, 1965.

Richey, Jeff, "Confucius." In *Internet Encyclopedia of Philosophy,* edited by James Feiser and Bradley Dowden. Online: http://www.iep.utm.edu/confuciu/.

Rosenberg, Matt. "Largest Cities in the World: List One." November 11, 2010. About. com Guide. Online: http://geography.about.com/od/urbaneconomicgeography/a/agglomerations.htm/.

Rosenlee, Li-hsiang Lisa. *Confucianism and Women: A Philosophical Interpretation.* SUNY Series in Chinese Philosophy and Culture. Albany: State University of New York Press, 2006.

Ruether, Rosemary Radford. *Introducing Redemption in Christian Feminism.* Cleveland: Pilgrim, 2000.

Schmid, Andre K. *Korea between Empires, 1895–1919.* Studies of the East Asian Institue. New York: Columbia University Press, 2002.

Schneiders, Sandra. "God Is More Than Two Men and a Bird." *US Catholic* (May 1990) 20–27.

Scott, Alex. "Emmanuel Levinas's *Totality and Infinity.* Review of *Totality and Infinity: An Essay on Exteriority,* by Emmanuel Levinas." Online: http://www.angelfire.com/md2/timewarp/levinas.html.

Shin, Gi-Wook, and Michael Robinson, editors. *Colonial Modernity in Korea.* Harvard East Asian Monographs 184. Cambridge: Harvard University Asia Center, distriubted by Harvard University Press, 1999.

Shin, Ch'ae-ho, and ŬlByŏng Chang. "Shin Ch'ae-ho's Nationalism and Anarchism." *Korea Journal* 26/11 (November 1986) 21–40.

Soh, C. Sarah. *The Comfort Women: Sexual Violence and Postcolonial Memory in Korea and Japan.* Worlds of Desire: The Chicago Series on Sexuality, Gender, and Culture. Chicago: University Of Chicago Press, 2009.

Soskice, Janet Martin. "Trinity and Feminism." In *The Cambridge Companion to Feminist Theology,* edited by Susan Frank Parsons, 139–45. Cambridge Companions to Religion. Cambridge: Cambridge University Press, 2002.

Star, Daniel. "Do Confucians Really Care? A Defense of the Distinctiveness of Care Ethics: A Reply to Chenyang Li." *Hypotia* 17/1 (Winter 2002) 77–106.

Suh, David Kwang-Sun. "A Biographical Sketch of An Asian Theological Consultation." In *Minjung Theology: People as Subjects of History,* edited by the Commission on Theological Concerns of the Christian Conference of Asia, 16–17. Third World Series. Maryknoll, NY: Orbis, 1981.

Suh, Nam-dong. "Towards a Theology of Han." In *Minjung Theology: People as Subjects of History,* edited by the Commission on Theological Concerns of the Christian Conference of Asia, 55–69. Third World Series. Maryknoll, NY: Orbis, 1981.

Suk, Monica. "Matchmaking in Korea: Mentally Ill Grooms Need Not Apply." ABC News International, July 16, 2010. Online: http://abcnews.go.com/International/mentally-ill-korean-grooms--apply/story?id=11177251.

Sungkyunkwan University webpage. Online: http://www.skku.edu/eng/.

"The Symbol Mark of Daesunjinrihoe." Webpage. Online: http://www.daesun.or.kr/English/htm/main.htm.

Tao, Julia Po-Wah Lai. "Two Perspectives of Care: Confucian Ren and Feminist Care." *Journal of Chinese Philosophy* 27/2 (June 2000) 215–40.

"Tikkun Olam: Repairing the World." Post on MyJewish Learning.com/ (website). Online: http://www.myjewishlearning.com/practices/Ethics/Caring_For_Others/Tikkun_Olam_Repairing_the_World .shtml./.

Tu Weiu-Ming. *Confucian Thought: Selfhood as Creative Transformation.* SUNY Series in Philosophy. Albany: State University of New York Press, 1985.

Walhain, Luc. "Minjok: How Redefining Nation Paved the Way to Korean Democratization." *Studies on Asia: An Interdisciplinary Journal of Asian Studies*, ser. 3. 4/2 (2007) 84–101. Online: http://studiesonasia.illinoisstate.edu/seriesIII/vol4-2.shtml.

Weber, Max. *The Protestant Ethic and the "Spirit" of Capitalism, and Other Writings.* Edited, translated, and with an introduction by Peter Baehr and Gordon C. Willis. New York: Penguin, 2002.

Wilhelm, Richard, translator. *The I Ching: Or, Book of Changes.* Rendered into English by Cary F. Baynes. Bollingen Series 19. New York: Pantheon, 1950.

"What Is Won Buddhism?" Online: http://www.wonbuddhism.org/won-buddhism/.

Wright, Chris. *Korea: Its History and Culture.* 2 vols. Seoul: Korean Overseas Information Service, 1994.

Yang, Eun-yong. "The History, Basic Beliefs, Rituals and Structure of WonBuddhism." In *Encounters: The New Religions of Korea and Christianity*, edited by Kim Sung-hae and James Heisig, 73–74. Seoul: The Royal Asiatic Society, 2008.

Yoido Full Gospel Church. "Overview of the Threefold Blessing." Online: http://english.fgtv.com/gospel/threefold.htm/.

———. "Yoido Full Gospel Church Story." Online: http://english.fgtv.com/yfgc.pdf.

Yoo, Myeong-Jong. *The Discovery of Korea.* Translated by Un-he Paik and Debora Park. 2nd ed. Seoul: Discovery Media, 2005.

Yuan, Lijun. "Ethics of Care and Concept of *Jen*: A Reply to Chenyang Li." *Hypatia* 17/1 (Winter 2002) 107–29.

Index

Index